"Being president is a job for just one person. And for the next four years, that person is Hillary."

—Dan Rather
CBS Evening News

BIG SISTER IS WATCHING YOU

**Hillary Clinton And The White House Feminists
Who Now Control America—And Tell The
President What To Do**

TEXE MARRS

 Living Truth Publishers
1708 Patterson Road • Austin, Texas 78733

*BIG SISTER IS WATCHING YOU: Hillary Clinton And The
White House Feminists Who Now Control America—And
Tell The President What To Do*

Copyright © 1993, by Texe Marrs. Published by Living Truth
Publishers, a division of Living Truth Ministries, 1708
Patterson Road, Austin, Texas 78733-6507.

All rights reserved. No part of this publication may be
reproduced, stored in a retrieval system or transmitted in any
form by any means, electronic, mechanical, photocopy,
recording, or otherwise, without the prior permission of the
publisher, except as provided by USA copyright law.

Scripture quotations are from the King James Version of The
Holy Bible.

Cover Design: Sandra Schappert, Texe Marrs and Wanda Marrs.

Printed in the United States of America.

Fourth Printing: 1994

Library of Congress Catalog Number 93-86195

Catalog under: *Politics/Current Events/Issues*

ISBN 0-9620086-9-9

ACKNOWLEDGEMENTS

Many wonderful, dedicated, and talented men and women have contributed to this book. My wife, Wanda, deserves tremendous credit for her encouragement and for her incomparable administrative expertise. Sandra Schappert again demonstrated her usual high level of creativity in cover design and layout. Kimberly Reiley was a Godsend: She did an outstanding job in typing the manuscript, and she was a great asset in the editing and proofreading process.

I also wish to express my appreciation to other staff members of Living Truth Publishers. The caring professionalism and team spirit of Joe Saldaña, Nancy Lee, Gerry Schappert, Rusty Weller, and Terri McDowell enabled me to concentrate my efforts on the writing of the book.

A debt of gratitude is especially owed the many leaders of patriotic and Christian groups and organizations whom I've quoted in the book. Thank you, my friends, for your boldness and courage in standing up for our nation and our God. You have been an inspiration to me. Surely, the United States of America will not be vanquished as long as we have such brave citizens, imbued with integrity and led by a transcendent and greater power.

Other Books by Texe Marrs

CONTENTS

INTRODUCTION

Hillary Rodham Clinton is not just co-President of the United States—she's the real power in Washington, D.C. And to help her run the big show, Hillary has brought in some very unusual feminist "talent." A motley collection never before equalled in American history, Hillary's women friends include lesbians, sex perverts, child molester advocates, Christian haters, and the most doctrinaire of communists.

Here are just a few of "Hillary's Hellcats" profiled in this startlingly frank exposé:

❏ *Attorney General Janet ("Johnny") Reno* - *Big Sister Is Watching You* provides shocking, new evidence that she's a hardened lesbian. As a Florida state attorney, did she cover up voter fraud by crooked politico friends? Discover the *real* reason why this Duchess of Doom wickedly burned to death the innocent women and children at the Branch Davidian compound in Waco.

❏ *Dr. Joycelyn Elders* - As Surgeon-General, she's out to make sure that pre-schoolers and elementary school children are given condoms and instructed on how to use them. Was Elders appointed to her high position as a *payoff?* Did she cover up the negligent act of Bill Clinton's mother, Virginia, who, as a nurse anesthetist at a hospital in Little Rock, was accused of carelessly bungling an operation and killing a patient?

❏ *Maya Angelou* - One of Hillary's closest bosom buddies, Ms. Angelou was called on to be the Inaugural Poet. She's been highly acclaimed as the "feminist Robert Frost," and her books are New Age bestsellers. Problem is, her real name is *not* Maya Angelou. And some of those books she's written? . . . Well, they are different, to say the least. *Big Sister* reveals that Maya Angelou is, in fact, a former stripper, prostitute, and madam. Why, then, did a *Southern Baptist university* make her full professor for life? Any why is this same institution paying Ms. Angelou over $100,000 annually, though she teaches no courses, does no real work, and has only a broom closet for an office?

❑ *Donna Shalala* - The lesbian community claims she is their Amazon "love sister." As Secretary of Health and Human Services, she oversees a multibillion dollar budget larger than the national budgets of Japan and Germany. Shalala is the most vicious Christian hater ever to hold a top cabinet post. Bequeathed the title, the "High Priestess of Political Correctness," the radical Shalala is so politically correct she outliberals the ultra-liberal American Civil Liberties Union. She's also a director of the elitist-controlled Council on Foreign Relations (CFR) and is a member of the globalist Trilateral Commission.

❑ *Laura D'Andrea Tyson* - A former Berkeley professor, Tyson is the Chairman of the Council of Economic Advisors. She's a big fan of the failed communist economies of Romanian tyrant Nikolai Ceaucescu and Russian dictator Joseph Stalin. A member of the CFR and the Trilateral Commission, Tyson says Americans are not taxed enough.

❑ *Roberta ("Bob") Achtenberg* - Hillary's put this lesbo crazy in charge of *all* federal housing policies. While demonstrating at a gay rights parade, the militantly lesbian Achtenberg passionately kissed her female lover as her young son looked on. Achtenberg once led a despicable hate campaign against the Boy Scouts. Why?—Because, she said, their oath includes the word "God."

❑ *Ruth Bader Ginsburg* - Now it's Hillary's Supreme Court, thanks to her selection of femiNazi Ginsburg as associate justice on the bench of the nation's highest judiciary panel. President Clinton praised Ginsburg as a "moderate"; yet, she's in favor of legalizing child sex with adults; she wants a unisex military and has called for the merging of the Girl

Scouts and Boy Scouts. A radical feminist, Ginsburg was the general counsel for the ungodly, anti-Christian ACLU organization for over seven years. During those years, the ACLU fought to take Jesus and the Ten Commandments *out* of the classroom while New Age paganism and witchcraft flourished *in* the classroom.

And Then There's Hillary

Then, there's Hillary Rodham Clinton herself. She was depicted once as the "Madonna" by the *New York Times*. But why did the editors of this liberal newspaper refuse to print the facts about Hillary's secret funding of hard-core, Marxist terrorist organizations?

Big Sister provides convincing evidence that in the 60s, "Hippie Hillary" aided the cop-killing, radical *Black Panthers* group. Now she believes God *wants* her to kill babies! Is Hillary—as rumored—a lesbian? Why did her feminist friends in the White House present her with a most unusual gift: *a witch's hat*?

What dark power does Hillary exercise over her hapless husband, Bill? What's her real goal? Will Hillary Rodham Clinton's unbridled ambitions catapult her into becoming America's first female president?

The Women of the New World Order

Big Sister is Watching You unmasks the powerful White House women who are members of the conspiratorial Council on Foreign Relations and the elitist Trilateral Commission. It reveals the identity of the women who have been favored to attend the annual conclave of the notorious Bilderbergers, as well as those who are hirelings of the left-wing, radical foundations designed to promote the New World Order.

These women are not individualists. They are part of a long-standing, serpentine network of international revolutionaries and fascist ideologues whose goal is to end American sovereignty and bring about a global, Marxist paradise. For many years now, they have networked together, preparing themselves for just this opportunity.

To accomplish their objectives, they have repeatedly proven their willingness to use the same iron-fisted tactics employed in the past by other ruthless dictators, ranging from Romania's Ceausescu and Italy's Mussolini to Germany's Hitler and the Soviet Union's Stalin.

Totalitarian in outlook, the women profiled here despise the very foundations on which our founding fathers built this great nation. They hate the sight of *Old Glory*—the red, white, and blue. They sneer at anyone who demonstrates a belief in old-fashioned American patriotism, and they hiss at Christians who show reverence for the God of the Bible. They also heap abuse and ridicule on the dedicated men and women who serve honorably in our armed forces—Hillary's Hellcats want to pollute the military by integrating lesbians and homosexuals.

Not just politically correct, these women are *brutally correct*. They are the hard of the hard, the most militant of a militant and hostile generation. Spawned during the 60s in the age of the Beatles, gurus, LSD, and hippies, they are the misfits of American society. But now the misfits are in charge. The lunatics are running the insane asylum, and they're out to make us into the pathetic creatures they have become. They are the feminist vultures who flew over the cuckoo's nest.

Armed With Gestapo Powers

What is scary is that these powerful women, because of their high-level positions in government, now possess awesome Gestapo powers. If Hitler and his henchmen had even a tiny fragment of the computerized, high technology spy, surveillance, and torture capabilities of today's CIA, IRS, FBI, ATF, and DEA, imagine what *additional* horrors they could have wreaked. These women have behind them the full apparatus of government to enforce their dictatorial demands and strange sexual appetites.

The *femiNazis* control a heartless police establishment more efficient than Stalin's dreaded *Cheka* and more feared than Himmler's bloody *SS Corps*. They are running roughshod over the American people, trampling on our constitutional rights, employing ecological idiocy to grab people's land and property, and committing terrorist acts against horrified victims. The fiery Waco massacre—and the mind-boggling government lies and cover-up that followed by Janet Reno and her cohorts—exemplify the chilling fate that awaits those who refuse to go along with the dictatorial blueprint of these coercive utopians.

Witches Who Torment Others?

The corrupt women who now rule over us are a strange, modern breed of Orwellian females who fully deserve to be called Hillary's Hellcats. *Webster's New Collegiate Dictionary* defines "hellcats" as follows: **1**: WITCH **2**: one given to tormenting others; *esp*: SHREW.

A hellcat, then, is *"a witch given to tormenting others."* A hellcat is also defined as a *"shrew,"* a ferocious, rat-like animal expert at quickly darting back and forth while tearing an enemy to pieces with its fine, sharp teeth.

"Big Sister" is my term for Hillary Rodham Clinton and her pride of hellcats who, at this moment, are plotting out new ways of stealthily attacking and devouring their victims.

Has 1984 Finally Arrived?

In his prophetic novel, *1984*, George Orwell gave us a frightening image of government leadership run amok. He introduced us to a new language of *thought crimes, doublespeak, and newspeak*. Orwell painted a dark picture of an immoral, Godless society where black is white, and white is black, and where two plus two equals five, if those in power say it is so.

George Orwell's cautionary novel was first published in 1948. The year 1984 has come and gone, but it seems as though Orwell was not far off the mark.

Big Sister did not arrive overnight. Hillary and Bill have been practicing their political black magic and skullduggery for over two decades. By now they are well rehearsed.

Hitler's Nazism also had a long gestation period. From his days as a corporal in Kaiser Wilhelm's World War I war machine, Hitler plotted his path into supreme power. Then, in 1933, he burst upon the world scene as a national hero, a superman, a savior.

Just sixty years later, in 1993, Hillary's Hellcats ascended to their own thrones in Washington, D.C.

Has Big Brother, in effect, been demasculinized, castrated, and transformed? Not really. Yes, he has assumed a deceptive, feminine mask. But behind the facade, the governmental behemoth described in such startling terms by George Orwell is still a *psychopath*; he remains a seething dynamo of energy—a dark, brooding, evil force ready at any moment to explode.

Big Sister is, in fact, the feminine, flip-side of Big Brother, just as communism, with only a cosmetic makeover, becomes fascism; and political correctness, taken to extremes, becomes Nazism. If a person travels from any point on a circle of evil, he or she will eventually end up in the same place.

Not A Partisan Issue

Big Sister Is Watching You is not a partisan book. My purpose is not to tear down the Democrat Party nor build up the Republican Party. The present, perilous situation which confronts humanity is beyond politcal party affiliation.

In a previous book, *Dark Majesty*, I unmasked the fact

that George Bush, a Republican, is a lifelong member of the occultic Skull and Bones Society, pointing out the threat to our freedoms of this secretive group. In this present volume, I examine Hillary Clinton and her feminist associates, who, ostensibly, are Democrats. But the elitists who have engineered the world conspiracy have no formal party label. Their only party is *money*, their only commodity is *power*, and their ultimate objective is *control*.

Such infamous groups as Freemasonry, the Bilderbergers, the Council on Foreign Relations, and the Trilateral Commission are more than happy to admit loyal servants of any political party—or of *no* political party. It is a truism of modern-day life that no matter which party is in power in Washington, things always remain the same. The agenda and plan of the elite is consistently advanced while the lot of the ordinary American suffers.

If we cannot trust in our political affiliations, one might ask, in what or in whom *can* we trust? I am convinced that there are only two things which deserve our trust—just two things that should inspire our actions: (1) God; and (2) The Constitution of the United States of America *(in that order)*. To protect ourselves and our families, we must put God first in our lives and glorify his son, Jesus Christ. He, alone, is able to adequately and surely guide us toward victory. This is why the women and men of the New World Order are waging war against God—but they shall fail.

Second, we must always remember that the women and men who wish to strip us of our freedoms and merge our country into a collectivist, global society ruled by the rich are the enemies of our Constitution. Through their lackeys in the courts and in the Congress they strive to reinterpret and make void the Constitution.

As patriots, let us therefore commit ourselves to reviving and restoring the Constitution as left to posterity by our nation's founders. American freedom and liberty are worth fighting for, so let us renew our efforts and recharge our spirits for the long campaign which lies ahead.

PART ONE

Now Let Us Praise Big Sister

Interviewer: "Which writers influenced your political thinking?"

Hillary Rodham Clinton: "I was fascinated by Aldous Huxley and George Orwell. Both *Brave New World* and *1984* were scary to me."

> — Hillary Rodham Clinton
> "People Who Inspire Me"
> (*Parade*, April 11, 1993)

I n April 1993, First Lady Hillary Rodham Clinton discussed with *Parade* magazine the people in her life who have inspired her the most. When asked which *writers* had most influenced her political thinking, Hillary's answer must have staggered her interviewer.

"I was fascinated," Hillary responded, "by Aldous Huxley and George Orwell. Both *Brave New World* and *1984* were scary to me."[1]

Those who possess a keen insight into human behavior and modes of thinking have long observed that the very things from which, at first, people recoil from in horror and shock, nevertheless are often the same objects which, strangely enough, seem to compel and attract their attention. How else can one explain the current revulsion of—and yet fascination with—gory and scary movies?

Hillary says that she finds the futuristic novels by Huxley and Orwell both fascinating and, at the same time, scary. These are novels which contain the blueprints for sheer human terror and absolute totalitarian control. What is most interesting, indeed, is that, according to Hillary's own admission, these were the books which *"most influenced her political thinking!"*

If this be so, and considering the fact that Hillary Rodham Clinton is indisputably the co-leader of the most powerful nation on earth, it is essential that we take a close-up look at what the authors of such frightening—yet revealing— books were trying to warn us about. From that vantage point, we will also compare the elitist plan of Hillary and her associates to the events which Orwell set for that gruesome and yet cruelly fascinating year, *1984*. Could it be that we are now rushing back to the future?

The Plan: Gazing Into the All-Seeing Eye of Big Sister

In the curious, opening paragraphs of *1984*, we are introduced to the all-seeing eye of Big Brother:

It was a bright cold day in April, and the clocks were striking thirteen. Winston Smith, his chin nuzzled into his breast to escape the vile wind, slipped quickly through the glass doors . . . The flat was seven flights up, and Winston, who was thirty-nine and had a varicose ulcer above his right ankle, went slowly, resting several times on the way.

On each landing . . . the poster with the enormous face gazed from the wall. It was one of those pictures which are so contrived that the eyes follow you about when you move. BIG BROTHER IS WATCHING YOU, the caption beneath it ran.[2]

As the plot of Orwell's nerve-tingling book unfolds, we discover that an elite group of evil leaders has spent years to concoct a Plan which they are using, with devastating effect, to control humanity.

The would-be tyrants of 1990's America also have conceived a Plan to achieve *their* objectives. That Plan, set forth by the super rich conspirators and puppet masters who have chosen and elevated Hillary and Bill Clinton into power, has ten major parts, or planks:

1. *Christianity - Out*: True, Biblical Christianity shall be extinguished and removed from the face of the earth, for it is subversive and a threat. In fact, it is the *gravest* threat to the success of The Plan.

2. *New Age Spirituality - In*: The replacement for true, Biblical Christianity shall be the approved, New Age, feminist-honoring spirituality, focusing the minds of the masses toward worship of the Great Goddess. Absolutism is to be declared a heresy, diversity a virtue, unity of doctrine the standard.

3. *History Rewritten*: History shall be revised. The traditional heros of the obsolescent age are to be discredited, scorned, and cast aside. New stories and new heros and heroines shall take their place in the pantheon of world history.

4. *Homosexuality Made Noble*: Heterosexuality shall become, in the minds of the masses, abnormal and the male-female relationship undesirable. Homosexuality is to be the norm, and the lesbian and gay lifestyle the preferred choice for our youth.

5. *Patriotism Smashed*: Multiculturalism shall be exalted, and the masses will come to despise white, male-dominated society as a throwback to the failed age of militarism and conflict. The masses shall be taught to revile nationalism, patriotism, and family.

6. *Death Embraced*: Death shall be made honorable, even heroic. Abortion and infanticide are to be encouraged; penalties levied on birth. Life shall be diminished. Euthanasia shall be made into an art form as the elderly, no longer considered useful, are assisted in their "transformation into spirit."

7. *Children to Rule*: Children shall rule over their elders. "Children's rights!" is to be the rallying cry of progressive society. Youth and vitality shall bravely lead *homo noeticus* (the new, super being) into the radiant New Age of globalism and community.

8. *Woman to Dominate*: Women shall dominate in all walks of life—in law, medicine, literature, religion, economics, entertainment, education, and especially in politics. Democracy will guarantee this result, for women shall be lionized and advanced by a controlled media.

9. *Individualism to be the Enemy*: Private enterprise and initiative are to be thwarted. The energies of people shall be devoted to the collective community. Individualism shall be depicted as evil and selfish. Service to the community shall be the sole criterion for whether a person is deserving of tangible advancement and material rewards.

10. *Big Sister Exalted*: Big Sister shall promote the goals as set forth in this Plan through any and all means available. The police powers and apparatus of government will insure compliance. Thought and hate crimes by those less spiritually and culturally advanced shall be harshly dealt with, first by law enforcement authorities and then by counselors and facilitators trained in the newest, approved techniques of psychological health. Above all, resistance by the masses must be crushed—ruthlessly, inevitably, completely. The future shall belong to the conscious, superior race who know of and are dedicated to The Plan. For the others—the vast, helpless and pitiful majority who are trapped in their obsolete ways of thinking and reacting—the future shall be exactly as prescribed in George Orwell's vision of Big Brother's 1984:

> If you want a picture of the future, imagine a boot stamping on a human face—forever.[3]

The Reversal of Reality

This is a detailed blueprint for shepherding the masses (you and me!) into a nightmarish existence. We are to be led like lambs to the slaughter into an Orwellian, *1984* police state.

To get us there, as we shall see later in this book, all the elements of the totalitarian New World Order are already being implemented. *Hate crime, reality control, doublespeak, newspeak, doublethink, thoughtcrime, thought police, blackwhite*—these are some of the heinous, *1984*-styled techniques and strategies our insidious masters are using to manipulate and control our minds to create a slave state. Yet, they are counting on we, the people of this slave state, not to even be conscious that 1984 has arrived. As George Orwell warned, in the minutely controlled society of Big Brother, which now, in the 90s, has been feminized into Big Sister—man's ordinary sense of reality is reversed, so that:

War Is Peace

Freedom Is Slavery

Ignorance Is Strength

"If one is to rule, and to continue ruling," wrote George Orwell, "one must be able to dislocate the sense of reality."[4]

The Plan of the evil totalitarians who bring us Big Sister is designed to "dislocate" man's sense of reality, to plunge us, unthinkingly but somehow appreciatively, into a New Age. In the end, we are not supposed to feel and act like slaves, but simply to do our duty to the collective "community." *The final stage, then, is for conquered man not only to embrace and admire, but to love Big Brother/Big Sister:*

> He gazed up at the enormous face. Forty years it had taken him to learn what kind of smile was hidden beneath the dark mustache. O cruel, needless misunderstanding! O stubborn, self-willed exile from the loving breast! Two gin-scented tears trickled down the sides of his nose. But it was all right, everything was all right. He had won the victory over himself. He loved Big Brother.[5]

The Objective is Control

At the root core, then, of The Plan is *control*. The elite group of feminists I call Hillary's Hellcats are determined to control the rest of us. Control translates into *power*. These calculating and ruthless women are clever and diabolical enough to understand that only if the world can be transformed and molded into a *global dictatorship* can their control over us be complete.

A republic—the constitutional, American republic set up by our male-dominated founders—will not do. The U.S. Constitution diffuses power, reserving those governmental powers not specifically in the federal realm for the states and for the people. Washington, Jefferson, Adams, and the other philosophical and moral giants who created our constitution foresaw the dangers in a socialist, collectivist state. They respected the dignity of each human being before God and drew up a magnificent set of doctrines to guarantee to the individual freedom from the usurpation of power by an authoritarian dictatorship.

Hillary Rodham Clinton has been the prime subject for more magazines than any other first lady in history. It was in Parade magazine that Ms. Clinton revealed that it was George Orwell's novel, 1984, which "most influenced her political thinking."

Now come Hillary's Hellcats with their neo-Nazi theology, proposing to sweep aside constitutional guarantees for the individual and replace these protections with a new *social compact* more fit, they believe, for the 21st century. Their Plan calls for a New Covenant, a new "Politics of Meaning" as Hillary calls it, in which *they*, as our Nazi rulers, will preside over the socialist state and *decide for us* what our lives and fortunes shall be.

As the pages which follow shall confirm, America has entered a Twilight Zone period during which our constitution has been suspended and is no longer employed as our basic law. We are on a trek to an alien planet because our feminist leaders have launched Space Ship America into a new, *politically correct universe.*

The Fourth Reich of the FemiNazis

What we are seeing is an abrupt and complete break, or discontinuity, a separation, almost an earthquake-like cracking of the fabric of our national being. We cannot find in the history books of the American republic parallels to this new, politically-correct socialist state. But we *can* find it in the history books of another nation-state: *Nazi Germany*, in the tragic twelve year period, 1933 to 1945.

Hitler, Goebbels, Goering, Hess, and Himmler did not create just a temporary monstrosity. Theirs was a model for the eternal socialist state. Hitler called his movement *national socialism*, or Nazism. But clearly, when he employed the term *national*, Hitler was not referring only to Germany. Hitler's Nazi doctrines were intended for universal acceptance, and his "nation" was global. The masters of the Aryan race, the Nazi fuhrer preached, were to rule the entire earth, presiding as planetary gods over the fate of the inferior masses.

Hitler, therefore, conceived of a "New Order," destined, he believed, to encompass the world.

Likewise, the women of the New World Order are adherents

of *national socialism*. They are the glorified femiNazis, considering themselves to be the feminist leaders of a superior spiritual race which scorns such "outmoded" concepts as nationalism, patriotism, Christianity, and the stars and stripes of our American flag. Nationalism, they preach, is passé, unadaptable to the modern New Age. Patriotism is an evil concept, they growl. And a false, spiritually bankrupt Christianity, they say, is only one component of the coming New Age World Religious Order.

Their new spirituality is theoretically comprised of *all* religions and faiths, but, in fact, is based on international Freemasonry's ages-old theology of a superior *human reason*. Reason, as defined by the new femiNazis, is the religion for the New Millennium. It is the embodiment of a new, global mind and a global ethic. In the New Order, woman is finally on top. She is not a mere equal. *She is Goddess.*

The High Priestess of WomanChurch: Big Brother in Drag

Hillary Rodham Clinton is, for the femiNazis, the fleshly embodiment of their heavenly Goddess. She is the Madonna of the New Age, the High Priestess of WomanChurch.

If George Orwell were alive today, I have no doubt that his chilling novel, *1984*, would warn us of Big Sister. In *1984*, Orwell's Big Brother had a face but was not a real person. He was the embodiment of everything that the "*party*" stood for, yet no one had ever seen Big Brother in the flesh. Instead, he was the voice and the image on the telescreen, the grand leader of Oceania, the benefactor of the people, the victorious Messiah.

Then there's Hillary. We almost daily are bombarded with visual images of this White House Goddess for she is the darling of the liberal press and media. We are repulsed, yet drawn by her visage. Charismatic, sometimes smiling, often projecting an icy image of shrewdness and single-minded determination, Hillary Rodham Clinton is Big Brother in drag. She is in effect, a politically correct, transvestite

Big Brother who, like the original model, rules from behind the scenes.

Hillary, too, like Big Brother, is the embodiment of everything the *"party"* stands for. And that party is neither Democrat nor Republican, it's the *national socialist party*— the women-led party of today's raging psychopaths: the *femiNazis*.

Big Sister is not, however, just a secret society for feminist believers. Be assured that Hillary and the women of the New World Order are more than willing to include man in their visionary utopia. But man shall not lead the new country. Man shall be disciples and followers of *woman*. The ancient Goddess reigned over men and women, but hers was a matriarchal society. Woman retained control.

Hillary, Our President

The femiNazis *demand* our respect and veneration. They are demanding that we acknowledge their *power* and *authority* over us. And across America and the world, they seem to be getting what they want. *Esquire*, a magazine for men, named Hillary Clinton its *Woman of the Year* in its August, 1993, "Sixty Years of Women We Love" issue.[6]

Dan Rather, anchorman for *CBS Evening News*, in a fascinating response to a question put to him in Indianapolis regarding Hillary's role in Washington, D.C., stated:

> Being president is a job for just one person. And for the next four years, that person is Hillary.[7]

Other feminist leaders around the country are fast discovering just who holds the reins of power at the White House. Increasingly, they have come to the same conclusion as has "Mr. Liberal Media," Dan Rather. On April 6, 1993, fourteen thousand women turned out at the University of Texas at Austin to hear Hillary Rodham Clinton give her famous but odd "Politics of Meaning" speech. Attending

Hillary, the most powerful woman on Earth, sat with Alan Greenspan, chairman of the Federal Reserve, during her husband, Bill's, first State of the Union address.

also was liberal democrat Governor Ann Richards of Texas. Moderator Bill Moyers of PBS—yet another flaming, New Age propagandist—asked both women what it was like to *govern.*

Hillary responded, "I am—just to set the record straight—not really governing." The politically clever Ann Richards quickly interjected, "If you believe that, I've got a bridge I want to sell you."[8]

When her husband, legally and formally the President, stepped to the podium at a joint session of the Senate and House attended by the presidential cabinet, the nine justices of the U.S. Supreme Court, and the chairman of the Joint Chiefs of Staff, to deliver his first State of the Union address, Hillary was there, too. TV cameras recorded that Hillary Clinton sat on the front row. Beside her, by invitation, was Alan Greenspan, Chairman of the Federal Reserve.[9]

Bill did the talking but, as the Chinese proverb so sagely puts it, *a picture is worth a thousand words*! That picture of Hillary Clinton, the most powerful woman on Earth, and Alan Greenspan, the world's top representative of banking and finance, side-by-side, in unison, burned an indelible image in the minds of millions of knowledgeable and perceptive Americans and, indeed, in the minds of thousands of astute foreign observers.

This was the message: Hillary represents the ascendance and preeminence of Woman. Greenspan represents Money, the ultimate asset, which guarantees, to those who possess it, *control and power* over the lives of those who do not.

Hillary Clinton and Alan Greenspan together represent *Woman in Control*, the powerful and transformative idea that woman is at last taking her long sought for position on the globe's political, religious, and economic stage. Big Sister is born, and the world will never be the same.

PART TWO

Hillary Plays Hardball

"When Hillary leans forward, puts her elbows on the table in front of her and hunches her shoulders ever so slightly, this is international sign language for, *'Be Quiet.'* "

— A Presidential Aide
Time Magazine
(May 10, 1993)

What dark power does Hillary wield over husband, Bill? That Hillary is Bill's superior in politics *and* in marriage is a fact that some feminists leaders have long known. During the '92 presidential campaign, the glossy, feminist magazine, *Vanity Fair*, boasted: "It is Hillary Rodham Clinton, lawyer-activist-teacher-author-corporate boardwoman-mother and wife of *Billsomething*, who is the diesel engine powering the front-running Democratic campaign."[1]

Hillary, herself, though, is more modest and unassuming, at least she's eager to appear that way in public. She's willing to grant her husband co-president status. "If you vote for my husband, you get me. It's a two-for-one, blue-plate special," she told the press.[2]

In a special "Presidential Commemorative Issue," *Newsweek* profiled the major figures in the Clinton White House. Hillary was one of those profiled. "She'll be (Bill) Clinton's Jim Baker—his most trusted advisor, period," predicted *Newsweek*. "She'll give him discipline, force him to make up his mind."[3]

Come again? *"Give him discipline?" "Force him to make up his mind?"* That sounds more like the tyrannical coach of a professional football team than a wife, doesn't it?

Hillary Frightens and Terrifies Bill

Some of Bill Clinton's closest men friends have confided that, from the beginning of their relationship, Bill has actually been frightened by and terrified of Hillary. Jeffrey Gleckel, a buddy of Bill's since their days at Yale, recounts how Bill first met Hillary Rodham, his future wife:

> One evening in the Yale Law School Library I spotted Bill studying . . . Then I noticed his concentration begin to slacken and his interest to wane. It was becoming clear to me that Bill's focus was somewhere other than the Law Journal . . . I managed to sneak what I hoped was an inconspicuous glance to see what was attracting Bill's

attention. There seated at a nearby desk with a stack of
books and notepads was my classmate, Hillary Rodham.
After awhile, Hillary walked over to us and said to Bill,
"Look, if you're going to keep staring at me and I'm going
to keep staring back, we should at least introduce ourselves."[4]

At that moment, says Jeffrey Glekel, Bill Clinton was at
a loss for words and momentarily forgot his own name.[5]

Bill Clinton has also recalled that day when he and
Hillary exchanged glances—and names—at the Yale Law
Library. "I was dumbstruck," Bill recalled, "I couldn't think
of my name." The President went on to explain that he was
both "fascinated and frightened" by Hillary.[6]

Hillary has also put her own spin on the story of how
their romance began. Why was she so attracted to Bill?
Well, she relates, she liked him because "he wasn't afraid of
me."[7] Which leads us to ask, was Hillary such a fearsome
and terrifying feminist-liberal there at Yale that all the eligible
men were scared to death of her?

In any case, Bill apparently *was* frightened by Hillary,
but it was this very fact—her bold and aggressive, in-your-
face, "Ms. Ice" personality, and her domineering, iron will
that so endeared Hillary to young Bill Clinton.

Who Wears the Pants?

R.E. McMaster, publisher of *The Reaper* newsletter,
commenting on the peculiar dynamics of the Hillary-Bill
relationship, showed insight when he wrote:

> Bill has an insatiable desire for approval, as demonstrated
> by his constant need to talk, his wish to appease and
> please everyone, and his tireless escapades with women,
> both during and following the campaign. He is most
> vulnerable. But Bill Clinton never had a male influence or
> role model in his family that he could rely on. His mother
> was married five times to four men. Small wonder he's

indecisive. He has no ground, no sense of security. I grieve for the country because of it.

Hillary, the lawyer (her profession alone speaks volumes), literally wears the pants in the family. Talk about craving control and anger! Here we have it in spades! So here we have a polarity shift, a sex role reversal. When Chelsea Clinton was sick in school and wanted to take an aspirin, the school nurse required Chelsea to call her parents to get permission. Chelsea called her father, not her mother.[8]

McMaster's remark that Hillary "wears the pants" in the Clinton family has been echoed overseas. In London's *Sunday Telegraph* newspaper, a feature story on the White House "power couple," snickered that, "even some democrats claim Ms. Clinton is an Amazon who wears the pants in the White House decision-making process."[9]

In *Time* Magazine, it was reported by presidential aides that the phrase, "Hillary said" is equivalent to an executive order. The magazine also noted that:

. . . the First Lady plays an upfront, active part in the presidency, from domestic affairs to political strategy to speech writing, bringing to the table no apologies. In all but foreign affairs, she has emerged as First Advisor.[10]

Significantly, when her husband's standing in the political polls fell like a rock in the first 100 days of his presidency, indicating widespread public dissatisfaction with the Clintons' policies on abortion, gays in the military, and their broken promise of a middle class tax cut, Bill called first on Hillary to bail him out.

In April 1993, as a depressed and harried president sat with 15 of his top officials to assess the first 100 days and figure out how to fix things, a gloomy Bill Clinton told his aides that he wanted Hillary to come in and chair the meeting to provide leadership. Whereupon, Hillary emerged from a side office and promptly took charge of the meeting.[11]

Above, the Clintons toast their joint electoral success at a luncheon after the inauguration on January 20, 1993.

Below, Hillary whispers in the ear of her co-President husband. To paraphrase the famed TV ad, "When Hillary speaks, <u>everyone</u> listens."

When there's a meeting of top officials in the oval office, "The President sits in the middle of the table, the Vice President right across from him, and Hillary wherever she wants," says one aide. "And the refrain we have all gotten used to is, 'what do *you* think, Hillary?' "[12]

"She is very smart," adds another White House aide, "and so nothing gets by her. *Nothing!*" "As a result," he added, "some people are scared to death of her."[13]

Hillary does, indeed, instill fear and loathing, especially in *males* at the White House. Even the top cabinet heads are reluctant to cross her. And when she wants them to shut up, they do:

> When Hillary leans forward, puts her elbows on the table in front of her and hunches her shoulders every so slightly, this is the international sign language for, *"Be quiet."*[14]

In an interview with *Time's* Margaret Colson, Hillary said that now that Bill is president and she's his "advisor," she spends more time with him than ever. Before, Hillary explained, she had her own law office to go to; now, she's got the White House.[15]

The View from the West Wing

The *Wall Street Journal* reported that Ms. Clinton refused the traditional First Lady's office in the East Wing of the White House and opted for a *suite* of offices in the West Wing, where the "heavy hitters" reside—and the real decisions are made.[16]

Hillary realizes that her dominant role with Bill as "first among equals" is not the American way. After all, she never ran for office and received no votes from the electorate. Consequently, she has alternated between being Empress and being submissive wife. She is an agile actor who can play both parts quite well.

During the '92 campaign, Hillary offered a tray of cookies

to supporters, claiming they were the product of her kitchen work (actually, they were baked by Powell Weeks, a cook who works for one of Hillary's female friends).[17] To the *New York Times* living section, she contributed a recipe and she has also played the pliant and faithful homemaker and mother on many a network TV program.

Hillary: "I Would Crucify" Gennifer Flowers

But clearly, this is all for public consumption—to fool a gullible, traditional audience. At bedrock, Hillary Rodham Clinton is a calculating, militantly aggressive woman who knows how to smash and maul an opponent. This feminist can scrap and claw with the best of them.

Judith Warner, a writer who, during the height of the '92 political fray, wrote a flattering, *authorized version* biography about Hillary Clinton for mainstream publisher New American Books, admits that, "In the course of her varying campaigns, Hillary Clinton acquired a reputation with some people for being pushy, arrogant, and domineering."[18]

On the campaign trail, shortly after Gennifer Flowers came out publicly with her bombshell about she and Bill having a long-running, adulterous affair, Hillary was heard on the presidential campaign's charter plane ranting and raving. "If we'd been in front of a jury," Hillary huffed, "I'd say, Miss Flowers . . . I would crucify her."[19]

On CBS' popular *60 Minutes* television program, watched by as many as 50 million viewers, Hillary blurted out, "I'm not sitting here because I'm some little woman standing by my man, like Tammy Wynette."[20]

Ms. Wynette, who's been universally acclaimed by fans as the reigning queen of country music, was not amused.

Hillary has also made it known that she does not intend to sit back and let husband, Bill, run the White House all alone. She says that she will not be the kind of display wife who merely attends ceremonies and cuts ribbons:

I'm not interested in attending a lot of funerals around the world. I want maneuverability ... I want to get deeply involved in solving problems.[21]

Shortly after Bill Clinton was elected, Hillary told an interviewer that in four years she wants to be asked "what *I've* accomplished."[22]

Hillary in Charge of Political Appointments

From day one, White House insiders knew that Hillary was a force to be reckoned with. She and Bill "micromanaged" the Clinton transition, reported the *Wall Street Journal*, in an editorial by Albert R. Hunt. The most mundane decisions were made at the top.[23]

Larry Patterson, publisher of the hard-hitting—and highly recommended—magazine, *Criminal Politics*, discussed the absolute control Hillary has had over presidential appointments:

> According to the generally reliable Washington Times, the three armed service secretaries have not yet been appointed, because all candidates *must be reviewed* by Hillary Clinton!! As of February 16, only Sheila Widnall has been selected by Hillary Clinton as Secretary of the Air Force. She would become the first woman to head any branch of the Military Service.[24]

Patterson also intimated that the White House personnel director, Bruce Lindsey, had no control over sub-cabinet and other senior slots. "Lindsey," said Patterson:

> "... gets his instructions from a mysterious New York lawyer by the name of Susan Thomases (whom we believe is a contractor to Henry Kissinger). Therefore, Hillary Clinton and Susan Thomases are going to be in control of the appointment process ..."[25]

A Stooge for Kissinger?

Is White House insider and Hillary associate, Susan Thomases really a stooge for Henry Kissinger, himself reputedly (on good authority) a stooge for David Rockefeller and the Secret Brotherhood? Quite possibly, this is the case, because both Hillary and Bill are unquestionably the servants of a higher-level group of elitists—the extraordinarily super rich who choose the members of such organizations as the Trilateral Commission and the Council on Foreign Relations.

According to one source, Susan Thomases does, indeed, have almost legendary power to influence policy. Firmly ensconced in the West Wing, Thomases acts as Hillary's personal secretary, executive assistant, and confidant. When she speaks, people quake. Even Bill Clinton snaps to attention:

> Sharp-tongued and assertive, Thomases has a reputation for setting people on edge. She pushed Bill Clinton to make a major AIDS speech five days before the ('92 presidential) election, a move other advisors thought was risky. When Thomases insisted, aides tried to time the speech to get less coverage.[26]

The London, England, *Sunday Telegraph* was even more direct in its mention of Susan Thomases. After discussing the fact that Hillary Clinton herself can be prickly and tough, the newspaper snidely remarked, "Then there is the controversial figure of Susan Thomases ... who is Mrs. Clinton's unofficial advisor and confidante—and a lot more than that, hint the crueller gossips."[27]

According to other sources, Susan Thomases has taken a special interest in helping push the lesbian/homosexual agenda. She is also an ardent supporter of virtually unlimited abortion rights for women.

Is Bill Clinton Subservient to Wife, Hillary?

Bill Clinton has repeatedly stressed to anyone who would listen how much he owes Hillary his political success. He also is known to frequently complain that if he doesn't give Hillary and her feminist friends what they want, he'll be in trouble at home.

Tom Kean, the New Jersey Republican, recalls a few years ago going with then Governor Bill Clinton to lobby Senator Chris Dodd of Connecticut on behalf of modifying a day-care bill being considered by Congress. Marion Wright Edelman, Hillary's liberal bosom buddy who chairs a bogus children's rights group, the misnamed Children's Defense Fund, was in favor of the bill exactly as it was and wanted no changes.

"I can't go too far" in opposing this bill, a worried Bill Clinton warned Kean. "I've got to go home at night."[28]

Wiser words were never spoken, for there have been a slew of reliable reports from the White House that if Hillary doesn't get her way with Bill, she raises cain. Secret Service agents, the highly-trained men whose job it is to protect the president and his family, are extremely unhappy with the goings-on at the White House. They've leaked story after story to the press about how horrible it is to have to work for the Clintons. They say that Hillary is a beast who throws tantrums. She's been known to pitch ashtrays, overturn furniture, and scream the most obscene curse words at husband Bill, all within sight and earshot of the agents.[29]

Two Secret Service agents, veterans of the more dignified and quiet George and Barbara Bush era, became so distraught and stressed out by the Hillary temper explosions that they officially requested a job transfer out of the White House.

Here is how one investigator described the thorny, volcanic situation between the Clintons:

> The stories filtering out of the Secret Service and the Fraternal Order of Police (FOP) in Washington, D.C. regarding the private exploits of the Clintons are mind-

boggling. *Newsweek* reported that a Treasury Department official told the Secret Service to put a lid on its agents spreading the word regarding the Clintons, or the responsibility for protecting the Clintons would be assigned to another agency. That's how bad it's gotten. A marriage of convenience is putting it mildly. That's how black things have become in the White House.[30]

This same source also pointed to the jokes that were circulating in Washington about Hillary and Bill:

The jokes filtering through the grassroots speak to the reality of Hillary's dominance. Let's just run down a few of them: *"I don't trust the president, nor her husband."* . . . *"Why does Hillary Clinton have so many Secret Service agents assigned to her? Because if anything happened to her, Bill would become president."* . . . *"When Bill Clinton expresses his opinions, he qualifies them by saying that they are those of his wife."* . . . *"Reporters are having a field day in Washington these days. It's fun to cover the new leader of the Western world, and her husband.. .."*[31]

Hillary's strange and eerie, dark power over Bill Clinton also extends to his family. Insiders confide that Virginia Kelly, Bill's mother, has only been to the White House one time since January 20, 1993, inaugural day. And Hillary just happened to be out of town on a "business trip" that day.

First brother Roger Clinton has openly admitted that relations between Hillary and Bill's family have been cool as a cucumber. Hillary's arrogant, little rich girl, superior attitude does not sit well with Bill's Arkansas "down home" family traditions. Reportedly, Hillary is not eager to associate with a woman (Virginia Kelly) who bets at the horse races and is an Elvis Presley groupie. Meanwhile, Roger Clinton's cocaine escapades make him, in Hillary's eyes, a pariah. It's not that she has anything against cocaine and drug users—after all, many of her glitzy Hollywood pals are dopeheads, it's just that Roger got caught!

Besides, as Roger Clinton himself tells it, the relationship between Hillary and Bill's family was doomed from the beginning:

> She had a Chicago upbringing and we had a down-South, Arkansas Bible Belt-upbringing. It was fried chicken and mashed potatoes versus a concrete wall.[32]

The chill and separation has continued to this day, Roger says: "It's been a long time since either one of us has gone out of each other's way to contact the other."[33]

The Wicked Witch of the West

There is a consensus among Hillary's women friends that she's one tough cookie. How appropriate, then, that in a *Newsweek* account, Eleanor Clift wrote:

> At a private dinner party with friends in Washington, Hillary was toasted with a joke gift: a *witch's hat* in anticipation that she would be accused of being the wicked witch of the West Wing.[34]

During the '92 presidential campaign, Bush's campaign manager, Mary Matalin (who, curiously, married *Clinton's* top campaign advisor, James Carville, a few months after the election) had a photograph of Hillary as the Wicked Witch of the West posted on her office wall. It was captioned, "I will get you, my pretty, and your little dog too!"[35]

PART THREE

Rage of the Psychopaths

PSYCHOPATHS
In his 1946 NEUROTICA article
William Krasner saw trouble ahead:

No nation or culture consisting wholly, or even largely, of psychopaths can long survive. The psychopath is a disruptive, parasitic, immoral influence. Any group, while it may for various reasons support and even honor the psychopath, must fundamentally rest on a firm economy and a great mass of hard-working, responsible people to exist. Therefore, in direct proportion to the extent that the psychopath is tolerated, that his attitudes find support in the culture pattern, to that extent it is an unhealthy society.

I s Hillary Rodham Clinton in fact the *unelected* President of the United States of America? After many months of intense research and investigation, interviewing confidential sources and combing public (and private!) records, I am convinced of this very fact. Hillary is a power over power—she rules over Bill Clinton and is the unchallenged authority at the White House.

What's more, Hillary Clinton is not just a case of a strong and masculine woman nagging and controlling an effeminate, wimp of a man who just happens to be her husband. Hillary has her own secret agenda, and she has recruited and empowered a loyalist clique of radical lesbian and feminist women to assist her in carrying out that covert agenda.

These women friends of Hillary owe to her and her alone their allegiance. They know she is their superior, and they are confident that she thinks just like they do. All of these women are *"true believers"*—ultra-liberal ideologues fanatically devoted to The Plan of which they are each a part. Moreover, the women whom I accurately call *"Hillary's Hellcats"* realize that their joint agenda, The Plan, can only be realized by their banding together as one. They are a group of women united in a conspiracy to set up a New World Order—an order in which feminist ideals shall reign supreme.

Rage of the Psychopaths

Just what kind of new world do the Clintonista women envisage? Actually, we're already entering the outer fringes of their frightening, Orwellian society. What I describe in the following pages is only a glimpse—a foretaste of the awful future that lies in store for us in coming months and years if these ruthless women continue to get their way. So let's put on our 3-D glasses and peer into the repugnant landscape painted in such dramatic colors by the psychopaths now in charge.

Yes, these women—and the underling politicians and bureaucrats whom they dominate—are psychopaths. A *psychopath*, as defined by Websters, is a mentally and emotionally disturbed person who pursues "immediate personal gratification in criminal acts . . . or sexual perversion." A man or woman with a *psychopathic personality* may be exceptionally intelligent and yet be socially a misfit and unable to function in productive society.

The psychopath who possesses power and authority over others is a dangerous person. With no sense of morality, lacking compassion, and devoid of conscience, such individuals are capable of committing the most heinous and despicable of crimes. Psychopaths are also vulnerable to fits of anger, during which they are likely to calmly and dispassionately persecute their victims. This is a fitting description of Hillary's Hellcats, for they *are* angry women—women dedicated to totally changing and transforming society. Their goal is to rid the world of the traditional values, Christian morals, and male domination that they so furiously hate and loathe.

A society which tolerates and even encourages the psychopath is a society on the perilous edge of disaster. Read, then, of the rage of the psychopaths . . . and weep for America.

Hillary: On the Killing of Babies

A lone psychopath is dangerous, but a cooperating network of like-minded psychopaths who follow the lead of an even greater psychopath can be terrible beyond measure. Since Hillary Rodham Clinton is the leader and role model for the femiNazis who now affect America, our spotlight should first be focused on her behavior pattern and aberrational thought system. We begin with a glimpse into what Hillary believes about aborting babies in the womb.

The following is an account as told to *Washington Week* by Lurleen Stackhouse, who approached President and Mrs. Clinton at the pre-inaugural prayer service held at the AMEC church in Washington, D.C., on Inauguration Day:

"When the service concluded we were asked to stay seated until the President and Mrs. Clinton departed for the White House. However, as they walked down the aisle I stood and reached out for Mr. Clinton. 'Mr. Clinton, America must stop killing babies.' He looked at me with a blank stare on his face. I repeated this statement to him.

"Hillary (not hearing my comment) then came to give me a hug and I said (in a voice only audible to her), 'Hillary, it's against God's law to kill babies.' She stepped back, shaking and trembling, and then grabbed my arm. Her countenance transformed from a pleasant demeanor to the appearance of being possessed. Her eyes were enraged as she replied, *'It is God's law to kill babies.'*

"I drew back in shock at this blatant and revealing statement. I fully expected her to say, 'It is God's law for women to have a choice,' or other pro-death rhetoric. But no, she was bold and blatant. I would not have believed it if I had not heard it with my own ears. I walked out with General Colin Powell. As the Clintons got into their limousine I approached the car. Through the glass I continued to plead with Mr. Clinton to stop killing babies. Again, he had a troubled stare.

"But the killing will continue so long as there is no understanding among church people about holiness. It will continue so long as Hillary Clinton and company have their feminist agenda enforced. It will continue as long as Christians continue to be apathetic and non-resistant. It will continue until God releases His hand of judgment upon our nation. But in the end it must stop. Until it does, the voice of unborn babies will cry out for justice."[1]

Hillary: On Lesbianism and Homosexuality

The psychopath can appear normal and traditional, yet internally, be simmering with uncontrollable urges and passions. The true female psychopath who is, for example, a lesbian, may well tend to keep the facts of her perverted sexual orientation hidden and in the closet.

During the huge, gay activist "March on Washington" in the spring of 1993, a lesbian leader stood on the main platform before an audience of untold thousands of other lesbians and homosexuals and joyfully divulged this repulsive bit of information: "I'm going to tell you a secret," she said, "Hillary Clinton has had a lesbian affair. At last we have a First Lady in the White House that we can f . . ." (word deleted).[2]

Was this woman lying? Sadly for America, though this lesbian leader's allegation was detailed during the Rush Limbaugh TV program, and even though the entire city of Washington, D.C. was abuzz with people talking about it, *Hillary Clinton has never issued a flat denial.* If this was a lie, Hillary should have been outraged. She could have immediately called a press conference and adamantly stated, "I am *not* a lesbian. That would be wrong."

But, she did not.

Of course, this was not the first time that stories of Hillary's sexual orientation have been published. Jack Wheeler, for example, a respected investment advisor and political commentator, wrote in his *Strategic Investment* newsletter:

> My sources indicate that Hillary Clinton is bisexual and fools around more than her husband. The stories you hear from the Secret Service, detailed to guard her, are mind-boggling . . . It is Hillary that is pushing the White House's homosexual agenda.[3]

In her unflagging support of the lesbian agenda, whether or not she is one, Hillary cannot be accused of rebelling against her husband's convictions. The two are not at odds over this issue. At the fifth annual "Creating Change" conference held in late 1992 in Los Angeles by the militant National Gay and Lesbian Task Force, Urvashi Vaid, the task force's executive director, brought cheers from the crowd when she read a letter from Clinton in which the president-elect praised the hard work of the gay rights movement. Clinton wrote: "Without your support, our victory on November 3 would not have been possible."[4]

Now that they are in office, Hillary and Bill are squandering taxpayer's money to promote the cruelly deceitful, lesbian/homosexual agenda. For example, in June 1993, Clinton's Transportation Department spent $1,900 for a rally to celebrate Gay, Lesbian, and Bisexual Pride, complete with buttons that read, "Straight But Not Narrow." This, naturally was a slap at those who oppose the homosexual lifestyle. At the rally, Transportation Secretary Federica Peña told the audience that President Clinton endorsed the project.[5]

Perhaps Hillary and Bill should pay close attention to Isaiah 5:20 in the Bible, where God warns, "Woe unto them that call evil good, and good evil."

Hillary the Marxist/Communist

In its exhaustive report, *Secret: FBI Documents Link Bill and Hillary to Marxist-Terrorist Network*, Sunset Research Group of Wichita, Kansas, proves conclusively that Hillary Clinton has long been an ardent and committed supporter of communism, Marxism, and the international Marxist-terrorist network.[6] Put together by former intelligence officers, the group obtained FBI documents which reveal the most abominable atrocities by Hillary.

The FBI documents show that Hillary Clinton has had a long association, beginning from her student days at Yale Law School, with a pro-communist front group, the Institute for Policy Studies. As editor of *Yale Review of Law and Social Action*, Hillary urged "sympathetic understanding" of Black Panthers then on trial for murder. That same issue featured:

> Several drawings depicting policemen as pigs. One drawing
> is of rifle-toting, hairy-snouted pigs with nasal drip, on

formation emitting "oinks" and thinking to themselves, "niggers, niggers, niggers . . ." Another shows a decapitated and dismembered pig (police officer) squealing in agony. It is captioned, "Seize the Time."[7]

In the August 1992 issue of *The American Spectator*, an article by Daniel Wattenberg revealed that while serving as director and chair of the board of directors of the socialist New World Foundation in 1987-1988, Hillary Clinton praised and gave away significant sums of money to several left-wing and communist organizations, including the Institute for Policy Studies; the Committee in Support of the People of El Salvador (sponsoring Marxist, Salvadoran guerillas); the National Lawyers Guild, an official adjunct of the Communist Party USA; radical lawyer (the "Chicago Seven") William Kunstler's Center for Constitutional Studies; and others.[8]

The FBI papers show that among the groups endorsed and funded by Hillary Clinton were the most extreme Stalinist/communist organizations in the world. One group to which she gave money, the National Lawyers Guild, held a convention in Austin, Texas at which the delegates sang the communist "Internationale" anthem, whose lyrics include the verse, *"Tis the final conflict, let each stand his place. The International Soviet shall be the Human Race."*

Hillary, the records show, also supported subversive groups which aided the Nicaraguan Sandinista thugs, funded terrorist PLO leader Yassar Arafat, and backed communist North Vietnam during the Vietnam War.[9]

What is frightening is that the FBI has been investigating these extremist groups, especially the Institute for Policy Studies, for many years. But now that Hillary and Bill are in command at the White House, the FBI has been ordered to "cease and desist." Janet Reno, Hillary's attorney general, even fired William Sessions, the FBI director who had to have known the awful truth about Hillary's hidden connections with this Marxist-terrorist network.

But that's not all: Hillary and Bill have been recruiting

communists and other America-hating subversives for key administration posts, especially at the sub-cabinet level where most of the real work of government takes place.

Case in point: Johnnetta Cole. Hillary chose Ms. Cole to head the transition team in charge of selecting the people who would hold high offices in education, the arts, labor, and humanities. A butch-haired, African-American feminist, Cole, president of Spelman College, is a longtime friend of Donna Shalala, Hillary's Secretary of HHS. Johnnetta Cole also just happens to be a fiery-eyed, dyed-in-the-wool communist![10]

Cole is an admirer of Cuban dictator Fidel Castro. She was a leader in the Marxist Vinceremos Brigade, led anti-American demonstrations in the Vietnam era, and headed a communist front called The Committee to Stop U.S. Aggression Against Cuba. Cole was also president of the communist-inspired U.S.-Grenada Friendship Society.[11]

The *New York Post* reported, "Johnnetta Cole had exceedingly close ties to the American communist movement in the 1970s and 1980s. And there's no evidence that she ever experienced an ideological change of heart."[12]

As I mentioned earlier, there is little substantive difference between the Nazis and Communists. Both ideological groups call for hard-line, central dictatorial control. With Marxist radicals like Johnnetta Cole selecting the people who now lead the Clinton administration, America has moved further along toward *1984* and the perfected CommuNazi state.

Sadly, once our proud and free nation does attain that hideous state of CommuNazi perfection, its leaders can never say that they did not know what was going on. *They know.* Our congress is especially guilty and culpable. In a June 1, 1993, speech in his home district, Representative Richard Armey (R-TX), stated: "Hillary Clinton bothers me a lot. I realized the other day that her thoughts sound a lot like Karl Marx. She hangs around a lot of Marxists. All her friends are Marxists."[13]

Instead of being applauded for telling the truth, Congressman Armey was viciously attacked back in

Washington by other legislators. "Attacking the First Lady as a communist is absolutely despicable," exploded ultra-liberal Representative Vic Fazio.[14]

In response, a frightened Armey retracted his comment and apologized. As the maxim says, truth is the first casualty in a government headed by thugs and thieves.

Hillary and the CommuNazi Power Grab

Hillary has bluntly stated that the goal of the Clinton administration is nothing less than "the remaking of the American way of politics, government, indeed, life."[15] Hillary has purposely refrained from fully explaining in public what exactly she has in mind. But only 120 days after Hillary and Bill assumed office, George Will, in his nationally syndicated column, warned readers that there were scary dimensions to the new Clinton White House. "The Clinton administration's emerging self-portrait" he wrote, "is not a pretty picture but it is becoming clear. *It is a picture of an aggressive and comprehensive power grab.*"[16]

In a speech at the University of Texas at Austin, Ms. Clinton talked about her conception of the new "Politics of Meaning." In ominous tones, she announced, "Let us be willing to remold society by redefining what it means to be a human being in the 20th century, moving into the new millennium."[17]

How remarkable! *Remold society . . . redefine what it means to be a human being . . . the new millennium*—all catchphrases for a very, very dark agenda.

In a *Newsweek* interview, Hillary suggested that the country must be willing to take drastic measures, if necessary, to end the breakdown in law and order (curious words for some liberals, but not for a *CommuNazi* liberal!):

> I have advocated highly structured inner city schools. I have advocated uniforms for kids in inner city schools. I have advocated that we have to help structure people's environment . . .[18]

Is this a call for uniformed "Brown Shirt" brigades in our city? The Clintons have also spawned a plan for a national youth corps. Will this evolve someday into a 1990's CommuNazi youth organization?

The Clinton administration has also offered up proposals to set up a universal registration program for infants (ostensibly to enforce vaccinations) and to issue a "smart card" to every U.S. citizen (as part of the health care insurance plan).

Control of our lives—that's the intention. How pertinent, then, is this revealing quote from Professor Carroll Quigley's infamous book, *Tragedy And Hope*, in which he describes how the international conspirators will control we, the masses. And remember: Quigley was Bill Clinton's mentor when the young, future president was a student at Georgetown, a Jesuit university in Washington, D.C.:

> The individual's freedom and choice will be controlled within very narrow alternatives—by the fact that he will be numbered from birth. . . . and followed as a number through his educational training--his required military or other public service—his tax contributions—his health and medical requirements—and his final retirement and death benefits. . . .[19]

This is Wizard of Oz government without a heart and without a soul. Hillary Clinton has said that the goal is the "reconstruction of society."[20] Albert Weeks, a professor of politics and history at New York University and national security editor of the *New York City Tribune*, notes that this is essentially the same phraseology used in recent years by communist powers. The Soviet Union's communist overlord, Mikhail Gorbachev, spoke of *perestroika* (restructuring); China's red butcher, Li Peng, employs the same catchphrase, which is the term *kai tsao* in Chinese.[21]

However, most of the former Soviet Republics still have no true democracy. The same old hard-line communists are in charge. And in China, the massacre at Tiananmen Square gave the world a clear picture of the rigid limits on freedom set by China's "kai tsao" reconstruction of society.

However, we need not look overseas to see what is in store for us once Big Sister fully restructures American society. On April 19, 1993, in Waco, Texas, psychopath Janet Reno, the "Duchess of Doom,"* with the full approval of the Oval Office, unleashed her own version of the Tiananmen Square massacre. The shooting and burning of 86 innocent Branch Davidians by the Clintonistas in a SS Gestapo-styled raid was almost a carbon copy of the bloody Nazi assault on the cornered Jews at the Warsaw, Poland, ghetto in the 40s. The massacre of the Jews in the Warsaw ghetto occurred on April 19, 1943, exactly 50 years prior to the Waco incident.

Satan's forces have long sought to stamp out Jews and Christians, and David Koresh's followers claimed to be Christian but flew a Jewish Star of David flag over their compound. Occultists have a morbid and fanatical obsession with numbers and dates. Therefore, could the 50th anniversary date have been a mere coincidence?

Hillary's Personal Guru

One of the most profound abnormalities of the psychopathic mind is its inclination to latch its teeth, like a growling bulldog, onto an idea or set of dogma taught by a guru. Political and cultural gurus are common among Hillary's Hellcats. And who is Hillary Clinton's own, personal guru?

It appears that Michael Lerner, a left-winger who evaded the draft during the Vietnam War, holds that distinction. Learner, publisher of the offbeat, touchy-feely, Jewish journal, *Tikkun*, helped Hillary develop her "Politics of Meaning" and "reconstruction of society" themes.

In Marlin Maddoux's outstanding newsletter, *Freedom Club Report*, Marlin discusses the odd, guru-student relationship of Lerner and Clinton:

---

* In Part Five of this book, each of Hillary's Hellcats profiled are assigned what I believe is an appropriate nickname, or moniker.

"An ominous sign of the ideology-driven White House agenda is the relationship between Hillary Rodham Clinton and her newly-found political guru, Michael Lerner.

Lerner has recently gained some fame with articles in major newspapers, pushing what he and the first lady call "the politics of meaning." At a recent White House reception, Hillary saw Lerner and exclaimed, "Am I your mouthpiece or what?!"

So who is Michael Lerner? He is:

* A former leader of the Students for a Democratic Society (SDS), a 1960's mob of rioters, at the University of California at Berkeley;

* A former economics professor at Berkeley whom a colleague described as turning his class into "a little Marxist cell";

* A militant who once told a newspaper, "I dig Karl Marx," and posed in front of a communist flag;

* A man who got married to one of his students by performing the wedding ceremony himself, decorating his cake with the words, "Smash monogamy." The marriage didn't last.

But that's not all. While both Lerner and Hillary Clinton have tried to sound spiritual on proposing something called "the politics of meaning," what they mean is hardly spiritual at all.

Reading Lerner's quotes, he sounds like he wants to turn industries into worker discussion groups, schools into group psychotherapy sessions, and foreign policy into a big 1960's love-in. But at the same time, he and Hillary would keep the Bible and prayer out of schools, along with family values like sexual abstinence and the Ten Commandments.

The problem is seen in a 1991 quote where Lerner reduces all our nation's problems down to one disease-free enterprise. But both Bill and Hillary say they love this guy, so get ready for more 1960's radicalism."[22]

New Age Politics and the Psychopathic Personality

In his 1978 book *New Age Politics*, Mark Satin signalled the emergence of the new politics and culture typified by the Hillbillary administration. He wrote, "The new politics is arising out of the work and ideas of the people in many of the movements of our time—the feminist, environmental, spiritual, and human potential . . . and world order movements." It is, he added, a "third force in politics" and is neither of the right or left. It is, he said, a politics and culture "beyond Marxism" and "beyond liberalism," and it is destined to move humankind into a "higher consciousness."

Mark Satin's book is perceptive and accurately portrays the New Age politics of Hillary Clinton and her femiNazi network. Their goals are "beyond Marxism" and "beyond liberalism." A few Marxists and liberals, though misguided, are sincere in their do-goodism and really do want to make the world a better place. Not so the Clintonista demagogues. I am convinced that they seek only *power*: Power for its own sake. But they can't help themselves. They're psychopaths.

PART FOUR

A New Age Goddess in the White House?

"There seemed to be millions (billions?) of us, all moving up the side of a mountain, each carrying a lighted candle in our right hand . . . I looked up and back—and as far as I could see in both directions were men, women and children, and the fire from those individual candles seemed to illumine the world with dazzling light. As we all reached the top, a beautiful *Light Being in the form of a woman* raised her arms and spoke these words: 'The planet is healed.'"

— John Randolph Price
The Planetary Commission

S he's spiritual . . . and religious. Words like "God" and "heal," "transform," and "spirit" roll easily off her lips. But is her *God* the Jesus of the Christian Bible? Is her *spirit* the Holy Spirit sent by the Father to those believers in Christ who are born again? Is she out to *heal* the environment of Mother Earth, or to heal broken and lost souls, as the apostles of the early church labored to do?

The question, really, is this: Is Hillary Rodham Clinton a true Christian or is she a modern-day, false apostle, a "worker of deceit" as the Bible puts it? Do we have a woman of God in the White House . . . or a New Age goddess?

We begin our search for the truth by examining what is undoubtedly the most mind-jarring facet of today's radical, feminist movement: the contemporary revival and alarming growth of the ancient goddess religion. As we shall see, this means more—much more—than simply using the term "She" for God, as crass and crude as that may be. The goddess movement seeks to dethrone God the Father and replace Him with goddess archetypes of early Rome, Greece, Babylon, and Egypt.

But the old, feminine spirituality started long before that. It had its origins in the Garden of Eden, when a domineering Eve brought a docile and unmanly Adam into a conspiracy against God. Was that key event in human history the beginnings of what today has become a society dominated by Big Sister?

Adam, Eve, and Big Sister

Big Sister is the ominous, end result of a universal yearning by unstable, masculinized, dominant-oriented feminists to establish control over men and women whom they consider to be their social and spiritual inferiors. It is an image of a society dominated by women who are rebelling against God.

It is, moreover, the story of Adam and Eve reborn. It was the woman, Eve, who first communicated with Satan in the garden and who then partook of the forbidden fruit. She then persuaded the man, Adam, to eat of it. She was the archetypical leader of New Age woman.

All New Age women are consumed by the hunger of Eve to disobey God, to rebelliously pluck and eat the forbidden fruit and to convince men to follow their lead. Barbara Marx Hubbard, a Clinton political supporter who was nominated for vice president of the U.S.A. at the 1984 Democrat Party Convention, has written a revealing book, *The Hunger of Eve*, in which she proclaims:

> I have always identified with Eve.... Throughout all of human history, we have been reaching for this mystical tree. Now we collectively stand at this fateful tree, driven here by our hunger.... Together we can create new worlds of undreamt possibilities for all people. We stand at that point in history where the hunger can be fulfilled...[1]

John Randolph Price, head of the Planetary Commission, a New Age spiritual group based in Austin, Texas, which sponsored the huge World Day of Healing event in 1986 (also called Global Mind-Link) tells of his vision of a feminine, goddess figure who comes to lead women *and men* bravely forward into a New Age of politics, economics, and religion:

> In February 1985, during a group rebirthing session in the mountains of northern Georgia, I was taken back to just before this incarnation—then carried in the future where I experienced the most beautiful vision of my entire life. There seemed to be millions (billions?) of us, all moving up the side of a mountain, each carrying a lighted candle in our right hand. There was no effort in climbing the mountain ... it was as though we were on level ground, yet there was the sensation of moving up. At one point I looked up and back—and as far as I could see in both directions were men, women and children, and the fire from those individual candles seemed to illumine the world with dazzling light. As we all reached the top, a beautiful *Light Being in the form of a woman* raised her arms and spoke these words: "The planet is healed."[2]

Price's "Mother Goddess" has given him the inspiration to announce the coming of a new, golden age in which all of humanity will be one, in which existing religions will be transformed and all national borders erased. In his organization's bulletin, he declares:

> You are the Master Builders of the New Civilization, and our work shall not be in vain . . . A New World will be revealed.[3]

We Are Her "Magic Children"

In *The Great Cosmic Mother*, Monica Sjoo and Barbara Mor depict that a New Age is already at hand. The Goddess is here, now; she has returned, and the world shall henceforth be made whole:

> Women are designed by the Cosmos to lead the human world back, now, to the great celebration . . . We will return to the Goddess, the Great Mother of all life, as her magic children.[4]

Women Reinventing the World

At their inauguration, rock bands thrilled the Clintons and their liberal Hollywood friends with the old Beatles' tune, "Say You Want a Revolution" and Fleetwood Mac's catchy "Don't Stop Thinking About Tomorrow." This was a throwback to the magic of the 60's, hippie generation—the revolutionary generation of Hillary Clinton. In the 60s, the Hindu gurus preached of the Great Mother Goddess who would soon come to recreate and renew the planet. Now, in the 90s, according to Hillary and the femiNazis, she, the Goddess has arrived. The time for renewal—for reinventing—is here.

Rosemary Reuther, a professor of theology at Garrett Evangelical Theological Seminary in Evanston, Illinois, is one of today's leaders in convincing women that their time has come:

> Today, women are in the vanguard of the aborning civilization; and it is to the women that we look for salvation in the healing and restorative waters of Aquarius. It is to such a New Age that we look now with hope as the present age of masculism succeeds in destroying itself. . . . The rot of masculine materialism has indeed permeated all spheres of twentieth century life.[5]

"We Women Are Going to Bring an End to God"

Naomi Goldenberg, who teaches religion at the University of Ottawa, in Ontario, Canada, as a "feminist theologian," heartily agrees with Reuther. In her book, *Changing of the Gods*, Goldenberg sternly predicts the overthrow of the existing forms of both Christianity and Judaism.

"God is going to change," writes Goldenberg. "We women are going to bring an end to God. We will be the end of him."[6]

Happily, Goldenberg announces that WomanChurch will replace the obsolete Christian and Jewish faiths. And what *is* WomanChurch? *"Witchcraft,"* she responds. Witchcraft, says Goldenberg, "is a perfect substitute for Christianity."[7]

But, Hillary's fans may protest, Hillary has not advocated the overthrow of Christianity. She has not proposed an end to God.

Wrong. Hillary has, indeed, indirectly advocated the end of the patriarchal God and the overthrow of Christianity. In the most ingenious manner, Hillary seeks to give us an entirely new form of Christianity. The new religion approves the sacrifice of unborn babies, celebrates lesbian sex, and ordains marriage between homosexuals.

As Rosemary Reuther indicates, the "wise woman" knows

that a resistant humanity is not yet ready for the complete rooting out and removal of traditional Christianity. But subversion and sabotage by women and the men whom they dominate will fix that, to be followed by "a new kind of Christianity freed from the bonds of patriarchy and purified of the last vestiges of sexism, clericalism, and militarism."[8]

The Christian church is about to be *religiously cleansed* by the femiNazis. They may continue to call it "Christianity," for the shrewd and cunning leaders of WomanChurch realize that the inhabitants of the old world feel strangely comforted by words and language with which they are familiar. But the old faith will eventually be cleansed and renewed, being made ready for the New Age of revived, national socialism.

A New Holy One is Emerging: The Serpent as Goddess

Catholic nun Madonna Kolbenschlag is an advocate of the new, cleansed faith. In a blistering address Ms. Kolbenschlag gave before 2,500 other liberal Catholic nuns, priests, and theologians in Washington, D.C., she proclaimed that, "The myth of the Father God is largely a product of the Judo Christian tradition." This tradition, she exulted, is changing and now we are about to see a new "Holy One."[9]

To cheers and applause, she thundered this conclusion: "The Holy One," said Kolbenschlag, "is breaking through the conscious of humanity as the goddess."[10]

Hillary and her Hellcats no doubt see the new, fast-emerging feminist theology as an ally in their efforts to establish a collectivist global state ruled by women who hold positions of vast power and influence. But they better beware! The goddess is *not* God, nor is the God of the Bible willing to allow goddess worshippers to assign to Him a feminine name or image.

The frightening fact is that the goddess is simply the devil in a feminist guise. She is *he*, and *he* is the serpent.

It is no accident that it was the serpent whom Eve communed with in the garden. Nor is it coincidental that in a recent issue of a major theological magazine, a feminist theologian contributed an article entitled "Reclaiming Serpent Power." In the eye-opening article, Alexandra Kovats, formerly the program director for apostate Catholic priest, Matthew Fox's, Institute in Culture and Creation Spirituality, wrote:

> In Hindu and Buddhist India the elevation of "Serpent Power," the *kundalini*, is a leading motif of yoga symbolism. It is the tantric image of the *female serpent* coiled in the base ... of the spine.

> The aim of yoga is to rouse this serpent power, to lift *her* head and bring her up the channel of the spine to the ... crown of the head. *She* is a symbol of transformation ... as she moves up through the human body ...

> Befriending this (serpent) creature can add to our own process of transformation.... Each of us must reclaim the power of the serpent ... we can befriend the serpent to help us choose life and good ...

> I believe that it is time for us to reclaim the positive dimensions of serpent power in ourselves.[11]

Hillary, Jezebel, and the New Age Movement

David J. Meyer, a dedicated Christian who once was deep into witchcraft and occult astrology and is one of the nation's most knowledgeable authorities on the subject, has noted the striking, Biblical parallels between Bill and Hillary and Ahab and Jezebel. In the Old Testament, Ahab the king is shown to be a weak, indecisive ruler who is married to a tyrannical, determined—and thoroughly sinful—feminist queen, Jezebel. Everything Jezebel did was inspired by the devil. She wickedly conspired behind the scenes to defraud a land owner so that her husband, Ahab, could have his land. She also sought to murder true men of God such as Elijah.

Hillary Rodham Clinton, who has supported the bloody murder of unborn children and endorsed the sexual sins of radical homosexuals and lesbians, among other atrocities, does seem to be cut out of the same cloth as Jezebel.

Hillary Speaks With the Ghost of Eleanor Roosevelt

David Meyer writes, "In the occult, the female force is dominant."[12] Jezebel was a believer in Baal, the fire god, and in Ashtoreth, the Great Goddess. In this ancient (now revived!) occult religion, communication with the dead was practiced. How fascinating, then, were the many reports from the media on February 23, 1993, that Hillary Clinton regularly consults with the spirit of former First Lady, Eleanor Roosevelt, the late wife of President Franklin D. Roosevelt.[13]

Hillary herself brought up the subject of her contacting Eleanor's voice from the other side in a major speech she gave to her Hollywood friends and pop singing stars. The occasion was a gala dinner that raised money for a statue of Eleanor to be erected in a park in New York. According to Hillary, at first her discussion with the ghost of Eleanor Roosevelt was one-way—Hillary did all the talking. But eventually, Eleanor began to speak back, giving valuable advice and suggestions. Jeanne Williams, who writes a celebrity column for *USA Today*, described the affair this way:

> Hillary Rodham Clinton laughed when songstress Julie Wilson got a bit naughty. And the First Lady said that imaginary conversations with her role model, Eleanor Roosevelt, helped her get through the traumatic campaign year.

> Hillary said her mental chats with Eleanor were "one of the saving graces I have hung on to for dear life. . . ." She went from asking Eleanor, "Why me?" to "How did *you* put up with this?"

Then Hillary said she had "a wonderful revelation": "Eleanor shook her head and said in my mind, 'You know, I thought that would have been solved by now--you are just going to have to get out there and do it and don't make any excuses about it.' "[14]

Has anyone ever told Hillary that the Bible identifies necromancy—communication with familiar spirits from the dead—as an "abomination" to God (Deuteronomy 18)?

Eleanor Roosevelt: Communist, Lesbian, Radical Feminist

A glance back through history at the bizarre life of Eleanor Roosevelt provides unusual insight into why Hillary is so fixated on this former presidential wife, and why she considers Eleanor her ultimate role model. In the 1930s, Eleanor was the most admired woman in the world on 13 separate polls. Fortunately for her, the American people were never told about the *real* Eleanor Roosevelt, the First Lady who was:

The late Eleanor Roosevelt, shown here decked out in her finery for one of her husband's inaugural events, is still communicating with the living, at least that's what current First Lady, Hillary Clinton, claims.

□ a fanatic supporter of left-wing and communist causes and organizations (The Communist Party USA considered Eleanor their greatest asset).[15]

□ a fast friend of all the communists, socialists, radical poets, left-wing movie starlets, etc., of her day, many of whom she entertained regularly at the White House.[16]

□ a confirmed lesbian. In 1978, the Roosevelt Library in Hyde Park, New York made all of Eleanor's letters public. In one letter to her lesbian lover, reporter Lorena Hickok, she wrote: "Hick darling, all day I've thought of you and another birthday I will be with you . . . Oh! I want to put my arms around you, I ache to hold you close."[17]

Lorena Hickok actually lived in the White House with Eleanor, and when she was on trips, she, too, wrote letters back to her lesbian intimate, the First Lady. In one such missal, the perverse Ms. Hickok wrote: "Goodnight, dear one. I want to put my arms around you and kiss you at the corner of the mouth. And in a little more than a week, I shall."[18]

Hillary and Native American Shamanism

One of the hottest New Age fads today, in addition to necromancy and feminist goddess worship, is Native American Indian shamanism. It's all the rage among women into New Age occultism. Once again, we find Hillary at the vanguard of devilish practices.

In early May, 1993, in Billings, Montana, Hillary arranged for an Indian "spiritual healer" and shaman to bless and purify her. There she was, eyes closed, reverently bowed, as the witch doctor performed the ritual over her. This was just prior to a meeting of her national health care plan committee. Hillary even allowed photographers to record the event for posterity.[19]

A Native American "healer" blesses a reverent Hillary Clinton.

Is this type of holistic health quackery what Hillary has in mind when she says she wants to extend health care benefits to all Americans?

A New Age Retreat at Hilton Head

Hillary's New Age beliefs are also evidenced by her and Bill's attendance each year at the Renaissance Weekend, held at Hilton Head, South Carolina, a posh resort island. Several hundred specially invited guests annually meet in Hilton Head for this New Age retreat. The agenda includes numerous pop psychology and other thinky-feely, New Age topics.[20]

Among the participants, in addition to the Clintons: David Gergen, presidential advisor; Education Secretary

Richard Riley; humor columnist Art Buchwald; former Bush speechwriter Peggy Noonan (who reportedly gave President Bush the "1000 points of light" theme), and Olympic gold medalist Edwin Moses. Proceedings and comments are "off-the-record" and are kept confidential; otherwise, there would be plenty of embarrassment all around when ordinary America discovered how fruitcake and nutty its leaders really are!

A Mother's Day Present for Hillary

Another prime example of the religious bent of Hillary Clinton is her church affiliation. In Arkansas, while husband Bill was attending a Southern Baptist church in Little Rock and singing in the choir (to make sure that he was spotted by TV viewers, e.g., "voters"), Hillary doggedly refused to attend. Baptist churches, she snarled, were too dogmatic, too fundamentalist.

Hillary prefers the more liberal, social activist United Methodist Church and is a member of that denomination. But her *real* preference was made known on May 10, 1982, when her hubby, Bill, took Hillary to visit the Glide Memorial Church in San Francisco. This, she glowingly told reporters outside on the steps, was "the best Mother's Day present anyone ever gave me."[21]

And just what kind of church is Glide Memorial? Well, the church once hosted a national hooker's convention. The congregation is strongly pro-gay and has repudiated most basic Christian doctrines. The pastor of Glide Memorial has said he "is tired of hearing about Jesus."[22]

"In Truth, Lord, You Are My Mother"

The way things are going, Hillary's typical Methodist church may not be too far behind Glide Memorial in adopting New Age absurdities. In Louisville, Kentucky, this year, a Methodist General Conference endorsed a new "Book of Worship" for

America's 8.9 million United Methodists. The most startling new prayer, unearthed from the 11th century writings of St. Anselm, is addressed to Jesus: ". . . In truth, Lord, you are my mother."[23]

Given the fact that in the past she's endorsed the extremes of Mother Earth environmentalism, as well as Marxist ideals and the feminist agenda of her presidential cabinet girlfriends, Hillary would feel right at home in a church which addresses Christ as "Mother."

A Goddess in the White House

Berit Kjos, an authority on the burgeoning, new, Mother Goddess religion has stated that the Earth Summit held in Rio de Janeiro in 1992—endorsed by Bill Clinton and Al Gore—was a celebration of pagan goddess, feminist spirituality. "The feminist arm of the Earth summit," writes Kjos, blends all four pillars of the Green colossus: Marxist

Amazingly, the New York Times (November 11, 1993) published this image of Hillary Rodham Clinton as the Madonna, come to bless the United States of America.

idealism (and oppression), the illusion of peace, earth-centered spirituality, and feminist agenda."[24]

Kjos also reports that in Rio, when an African choir began to sing praises to God, Bella Abzug, the liberal, former Congresswoman from New York, cried into the microphone, "You mean the *goddess!*"[25]

Bella Abzug, of course, was an enthusiastic supporter of the candidacy of Hillary and Bill Clinton in the '92 presidential sweepstakes, as were all goddess worshippers. The vigorous, even fanatical efforts of these radical, God-despising femiNazis have been generously rewarded: Today, a New Age goddess sits in the White House.

PART FIVE

Bad Company

It used to be that we had to put up with the tuxedoed Council on Foreign Relations, Trilateral Commission, New World Order, and Internationalists. Now we've got to put up with the red hot *Revolutionaries* in the driver's seat!

—Charles A. Provan, M.D.
American Freedom Movement

ROBERTA ACHTENBERG

Position: Assistant Secretary of Housing and Urban Development

Moniker: *Queer Choice*

Roberta ("My friends just call me Bob.") Achtenberg is a successful starlet in her own way. She's starred in a very special movie—a cinematic extravaganza graphically depicting the excesses of "Gay Pride." Indeed, "Bob" Achtenberg seems to be the first pornographic "film star" to ever win appointment to a major government post—that of assistant secretary of HUD.

Achtenberg's starring role was her knockout "performance" in a 1992 video of a *San Francisco* Gay Pride parade.

That sickening video captures a scene in which Ms. Achtenberg passionately embraces and kisses her lesbian lover—a San Francisco woman judge.

This bizarre lesbian activist, Roberta Achtenberg, is demanding that queers be appointed Boy Scout troopmasters. She has also made vile speeches insisting that the Boy Scout organization be punished until it approves of the gay lifestyle and openly welcomes homosexuals as role models for young boys. Achtenberg was also angered that the Boy Scouts include a reference to God in their oath. That, she fumed, is unAmerican!

Promoting the Pedophile Agenda

This, of course, is all part of the radical homosexual agenda— to put pedophile child molesters in key positions in youth organizations such as the Boy Scouts. Achtenberg, no doubt, will squirm and deny this is also her objective, but such perverted groups as the North American Man/Boy Love

Association (NAMBLA) are wildly supportive of Achtenberg's position. NAMBLA's motto is "sex before eight or it's too late."

Here's how one perceptive columnist, Suzanne Fields of the *LA Times Syndicate*, characterized Ms. Achtenberg's hostile, "in your face," lesbian lifestyle:

> Forget what you may think about lesbianism. Forget whether you care if Heather has two mommies. Forget all the intellectual issues that define this debate.
>
> What do you think about two women riding in a convertible with the top down, kissing each other passionately on the mouth, while the 7-year-old son of one of them sits in the back seat, watching in bewilderment? What do you think when you see that the car carries a banner "Celebrating family values?"
>
> How do you feel that one of these women was confirmed by the Senate as an assistant secretary of the Department of Housing and Urban Development?
>
> Sen. Barbara Boxer, the California Democrat who led the floor fight for confirming Roberta Achtenberg, one of the heavy kissers, defended her because she thinks public policy qualifications should be judged as different from "homosexual lifestyle."
>
> Fair enough. But don't character and moral issues make up a person's qualifications, too?
>
> The kissers are from a 1992 video of the San Francisco Gay Pride parade; another scene portrayed a white-haired "God" in anal intercourse with "Uncle Sam." Their sign reads: "One nation under God."
>
> Our society has moved from taking pride in moral righteousness to a disdain for anyone who espouses virtue.

In 40 years, homosexuals have moved from rhetoric calling for them to blend into society, to become part of the power structure, to uncompromising visibility and "in your face" public sexuality.

It's precisely such observations that cause concern about Roberta Achtenberg's prominence and power. As a member of the San Francisco Board of Supervisors, she voted to bar the Boy Scouts from holding meetings of their troops in public schools because they refused to allow gays.

Robert Achtenberg's confirmation has been hailed as a breakthrough—the highest federal appointment for a lesbian activist. Dare we care if her attitude is, "in your face?"[1]

Please note that Suzanne Fields is in a very tiny minority as a conservative, pro-morality national columnist. In fact, hers was one of the only voices heard across the nation in the secular media which registered alarm at Hillary and Bill's selection of Roberta Achtenberg for this ultra-sensitive government post.

Another small but significant protest can be found in the superb little book, *Shafted! Bill and Hillary's Excellent Adventure*, written in political cartoon style by Dick Hafer. Hafer writes that Bill Clinton "seems to be determined to rub the noses of traditional morality citizens into his homosexual policies. He had 13 open gays high on his transition team, and Ms. (Miss? Mr.?) Achtenberg is the highest ranking open lesbian ever appointed."[2]

"She attacked funding for the Boy Scouts while on the S.F. (San Francisco) city council," Hafer adds. "Her 'partner' is a San Francisco municipal court judge. They have a son. How, for Pete's sake?"[3]

Lesbian revolutionary Achtenberg showed up for her Senate confirmation hearing arm-in-arm with her "lover" and even arrogantly introduced her to the senators. Only one of the senators on the panel openly voiced an objection, Senator Jesse Helms (R-NC). Helms remarked that

Achtenberg's flaunting of her gay lifestyle flew in the face of the majority of Americans. Naturally, Helm's comments were ridiculed and scorned by the television news reporters and by the major newspapers.[4]

Achtenberg's Mighty and Bloody Sword

As the top official at HUD in charge of enforcing the entire nation's fair housing and discrimination policies, Roberta Achtenberg is now able to wield a mighty and bloody sword against the traditional values of Americans which she so obviously despises. Decline to rent your upstairs bedroom, your duplex, or your apartment to the most disgustingly open homosexual and lesbian couple, and you'll most likely be in hot water from Roberta Achtenberg's goon squads.

You better believe that she already has militant, pro-homosexual activists, federal investigators, and the whole private homosexual gestapo out in force looking for violators of the "new porno sex religion" sponsored by Hillary and her Hellcats.

Remember, as explained earlier, the word "Hellcats" is defined by Webster's as "a witch who torments others." Over the next several years, Hillary and her pal hellcat, Roberta Achtenberg, will have their fair housing police descending on ordinary America like the voraciously hungry locusts of the biblical book of Revelation. They shall be our tormentors.

MADELEINE ALBRIGHT

Position: U.S. Ambassador to the United Nations (UN)

Moniker: *Madame New World Order*

An outsider to liberal, conspiratorial politics Madeleine Albright is not. When Hillary and Bill tapped Ms. Albright for the post of U.S. Ambassador to that bastion of global correctness, the United Nations, she was already well known among the Washington, D.C. international set.

Albright, 55, like a number of others on the Clintonista team, is a Jimmy Carter administration retread. As one foreign affairs analyst privately confided to me:

> Madeleine Albright and dozens more were responsible for the overthrow of conservative Prime Minister Ian Smith and the installation of the communist regime in Rhodesia (now Zimbabwe); they helped overthrow Somoza and install the communist Sandinistas in Nicaragua; supported the communist MPLA in Angola, the communist Frelino in Mozambique, and the communist ANC in South Africa; tried to overthrow the pro-western Pinochet government in Chile; gave away the Panama Canal, and opened the door to massive KGB, GRU, and DGI penetration.

> In short, America now has the most dangerous foreign policy team in history—designed to completely disarm us and take us post-haste into the New World Order.[1]

Madeleine Albright is a Democrat Party hack of long standing. She was deeply immersed in presidential candidate Michael Dukakis' 1988 bid for the White House and also was active in the failed campaigns of former Senator Edmund Muskie and vice presidential nominee Geraldine Ferraro in 1984.

The New World Order Connection

Ms. Albright is also one of the women of the Council on Foreign Relations (CFR) and Trilateral Commission (TLC), proof positive (as if any *additional* assurance is necessary given her sterling, liberal Democrat qualifications) that she will closely hew to the doctrinaire, globalist/socialist line of her CFR/TLC overlords.[2]

However, what must have made Madeleine Albright especially appealing to Hillary and Bill's left-wing radical tastes is Albright's professional connection with Georgetown University—Bill's *alma mater*. Georgetown, a Catholic Jesuit school, has long been a hotbed of Marxist ideology and a seeding ground for Liberation Theology, the strange, pro-Fidel Castro brand of insane revolutionary fervor spread by liberal Jesuit priests in Nicaragua, El Salvador, and throughout Central and South America.

As a Georgetown professor of international affairs, Madeleine Albright was right there in the same department where Professor J. Carrol Quigley once held sway in the 1960s, back when William Jefferson Clinton was a student. In his summer, 1992 speech in Madison Square Garden accepting the Democrat Party's nomination for President of the United States, Clinton openly acknowledged Professor Quigley's contributions to Clinton's own "enlightened" view of globalism and world citizenship *vis à vis* the old, "outmoded" concept of nationalism and American sovereignty.

Quigley, of course, was Bill Clinton's mentor at Georgetown. The professor wrote a stunningly frank book in 1966—the very year when young Bill was attending Professor Quigley's wildly popular—though leftist-oriented—lectures. The book surprisingly revealed the existence of an international conspiracy of rich elitists plotting a New World Order. In the book, *Tragedy and Hope*, Professor Quigley wrote:

> Their aim is nothing less than to create a world system of financial control in private hands able to dominate the political system of each country and the economy of the world as a whole.[3]

Quigley stated in his book that he had personal knowledge of the conspirators and their plan because he had associated with them for over 20 years. For two years, Quigley confided, he had been given access to their most secret records. He *approved* of their aims.[4]

Professor Carrol Quigley's *Tragedy and Hope* evidently revealed far too much. It also created such a stir among believers in a world conspiracy that the publisher, Macmillan, was forced to withdraw it from the marketplace. The book has now been officially declared out-of-print and is very difficult to find. Reportedly, a few patriotic organizations, in their desire to get the word out about this extreme, present danger to American sovereignty, have privately distributed a number of small, pirated printings.

The highly regarded Dr. Charles A. Provan, head of the *American Freedom Movement*, wrote this about Albright in his insightful—and highly recommended—monthly newsletter:

> UN Ambassador Madeleine Albright is (as you guessed) a member of the CFR. She was president of Georgetown University's Center for Policy Studies, was an advisor to Geraldine Ferraro and Walter Mondale, and was Mike Dukakis' top foreign policy advisor. She is a complete soft-liner regarding foreign policy.[5]

Dr. Charles Provan's knowledgeable observation about Albright's penchant for being a "soft-liner regarding foreign policy" is right on target. In the past, liberal left-wingers like Albright consistently opposed U.S. intervention in Vietnam, Cambodia, Nicaragua, El Salvador, Grenada, and Panama. But of course, that was when the big Soviet bug-a-bear was capitalism's archenemy. Back then it was extremely fashionable among the liberal intelligentsia to berate American presidents for their support of increased defense spending and to pillory and defame conservatives as imperialist "warmongers" and "global troublemakers."

United Nations "GloboCop"

Now things have changed dramatically. The New World Order philosophy of the Clintonistas requires that the U.S.A. cheerily become the United Nations' "GloboCop," enthusiastically willing to send its troops into harm's way wherever nationalist and anti-globalist tendencies raise their ugly heads. Since terms like "commie butcher," "tinhorn dictator" and even "guerilla hero" are now considered hopelessly passé and deemed politically incorrect, a new language is being created by the Clintonistas to characterize the heads of the newly discovered, local opposition to imposition of the New World Order regime. The term "war lord," for example, now replaces "Marxist revolutionary" and "ethnic cleansing" suffices nicely for "communist purges."

Albright, according to at least one report, is finding it tough to adjust to the new language and changed policies. She appears to be afflicted with a 60's malaise which makes her blink and stutter when making speeches at the UN endorsing interventionist, military solutions to local problems in Somalia, Iraq, Bosnia, and elsewhere. She's also in a particularly unsatisfying hard place because the UN representatives of the Third World countries are, by now, painfully aware of the dangers to their sovereignty resulting from the new, militaristic, GloboCop strategies of the Clintonistas and their super rich New World Order bosses.[6]

Newsweek magazine, describing Albright as an instinctive "Do-gooder," recently penned this cryptic comment about her lackluster performance at the UN: "Finding the United Nations tough to master (Albright is) torn between the interventionist approach and the skepticism of UN Security Council Colleagues."[7]

Perhaps the most intriguing description of the political inclinations and associations of Madeleine Albright comes from Franklin Sanders, astute publisher of the excellently researched and thoughtful newspaper, *The Moneychanger*. Sanders is also the author of a thought-provoking, futuristic novel *Heiland*. The fascinating plot of this book, though written long before Hillary and Bill assumed their thrones on January 20, 1993, as America's closest thing to royalty, seems to be chillingly reminiscent of what is now taking place in this nation, thanks to the Clintonistas. Franklin Sanders provides us keen insight into what makes Madeleine Albright tick:

> She's the daughter of Czech communist Joseph Kerbel, who became involved in an internal split in the Czech communist party and so took political asylum in the United States after working for the UN (1948).
>
> Albright served as president of the Center for National Policy and was a former professor of Georgetown University's School of Foreign Service, *alma mater* of Clinton and long home to Professor Carroll Quigley, establishment historian and Clinton mentor. A Carter administration retread, she worked for Mr. Consonant, Zbigniew Brzezinski, at the National Security Council, 1978-1981.[8]

Albright and the Trilateral Commission

Zbigniew Brzezinski, you may recall, was the man who, in the early 1970s, so inspired banker David Rockefeller with his book, *Between Two Ages*, that Rockefeller was led to organize and found the globalist-promoting Trilateral Commission.[9] And to think that Madeleine Albright was right there at Brzezinski's side at the influential National Security Council as he formulated and executed President Jimmy Carter's foreign policy for the United States! Now doesn't *that* give us great confidence that she'll adhere to a traditionally conservative and constitutional role in her current job as Clinton's UN mouthpiece?

JANE ALEXANDER

Position: Chairperson, National Endowment for the Arts

Moniker: *Czarina of Homoerotic Art*

Twenty million desperate Americans are now out of work, tens of thousands are homeless, a pitiful few of our 250 million citizens can afford health care, and many children go to bed hungry each night. But does the federal government have enough money to take care of all these terribly pressing problems? Of course not, even though the Hillbillary administration just whacked American taxpayers to the tune of an additional $500 billion.

But while our esteemed, liberal leadership in Washington, D.C. has little left in the kitty to take care of *legitimate human needs*, it has set aside a rather generous $178 million in the budget this fiscal year to fund homoerotic and other pornographic "works" of art! Yes, that's right—our president and congress have $178 million of funny money to dole out as they see fit to a motley crew of New Age, radical-liberal artists.

Of course, Christian and patriotic painters, sculptors, folk artists and so on need not apply. Norman Rockwell types are *verboten*. Only the sexually and religiously bizarre and weird and the angrily anti-patriotic Bohemians can get hold of this free money. Yes, indeed, if you're either a far out "artist" who's a Jesus-hater or you're a vicious homosexual "artist" who just loves to hate conservatives of all stripes, *Aunt Samantha* (didn't you know, "Uncle Sam" is out—*he's* politically incorrect) has some good news for you: You might just be eligible for some big bucks!

If you want some of this politically correct largesse, you'll need to get in touch with *Jane Alexander*. She's Hillary and Bill's choice to head the culturally progressive

National Endowment for the Arts (NEA) into the homosexually inspired New Age world.

Sex Organs and Rosary Beads

In years past, the NEA became embroiled in controversy as George Bush's own liberal chairman, John Frohnmayer, went around funding every type of blasphemous and homosexually dirty art project he could find out about. For example, there was the homosexual, erotic exhibit in Orlando entitled "Scents and Shivers." This rather unusual exhibit included such "art" images as male sex organs draped with rosary beads. One of the exhibits showed two gay men embracing in bed and swaddled in an American flag while wearing a crown of thorns—obviously a heinously tragic, blasphemous reference to Jesus Christ and an intended insult to American patriotism.[1]

An NEA grant of $15,000 went to a nude stripper named Annie Sprinkle whose live performances on stage sporting only a flashlight to illuminate the crevices of her naked body were paid for by you and me and every other taxpayer. Sprinkle, a self-proclaimed "Red Witch," boasted to a D.C. theater audience that the government was footing the bill for her "artsy" performance. The adoring crowd lapped it up.[2]

Another NEA bag of money went to an artist named Serrano who had a neat idea for a newfangled piece of art. Serrano filled a vat with urine and submerged a picture of "Jesus Christ" into it. He titled his masterpiece "Piss Jesus." The liberal crowd thought this, too, was simply marvelous.[3]

This monstrosity and dozens more like it were never exposed by the mass media, controlled as they are by liberal looney-tunes. But an avalanche of protest went forward to congress anyway from millions of little people—concerned Christians who learned of this terrible situation mostly from small Christian ministries, fundamentalist Christian pastors, and publishers of patriotic, conservative newsletters. Patrick Buchanan helped a bit, too, by criticizing the NEA's art funding during his bid for the Republican nomination in the '92 presidential campaign.

A frightened congress, startled by the depth of anger and disgust being demonstrated by ordinary (i.e., non-liberal) America, debated mightily in the halls of the legislative bodies as to the merits of this immoral swamp called "diverse art." As a result, a few meager gains were made by the Christian and morality forces, primarily regulations restricting the NEA from funding the most blatant type of anti-Christian, pornographic art. The liberal and socialist arts community was outraged. How dare anyone tell *them* how to spend the *taxpayer's* money! Censors! Bigots! Homophobic pigs! That's what the Americans are who believe in traditional values!

Bill and Al Sponsor Porno Art

Being the great and virtuous Christians that Hillary and Bill Clinton are, you are probably thinking about now that, being apprised of such horrific plundering of the people's treasury by blasphemous artists whose works are funded by a government agency, the dynamic duo would have vowed, "No more will taxpayer's hard-earned dough go for these vulgar atrocities." You would also think that the Clintonistas would favor "content restrictions" to block some of the more crude art being funded. Wrong! Indeed, Hillary and Bill have, on numerous public occasions, *applauded* the use of federal monies for such "enlightened" art projects.

The Clintonista policy on this vital issue, set forth during the '92 presidential campaign and published in the Clinton-Gore book, *Putting People First*, is as follows:

> We believe that the arts should play an essential role in education and enriching all Americans. We will help the arts become an integral part of education in every community, broadening the horizons of our children and preserving our valuable cultural heritage. A Clinton-Gore Administration will ensure access to the arts for all of our citizens.

As President and Vice President, we will defend freedom of speech and artistic expression by opposing censorship or "content restrictions" on grants made by the National Endowment for the Arts. We will continue federal funding for the arts and promote the full diversity of American culture, recognizing the importance of providing all Americans with access to the arts.[4]

Clinton is affirming here his commitment to fully fund, from the coffers of a bankrupt, deficit-ridden federal treasury, sick and disgusting satanic and pornographic "art" so that America's "valuable cultural heritage" will be preserved! George Orwell's insights in *1984* on "doublespeak" were again proven prophetic. It was also Orwell who, forty-five years ago in an essay on the depraved art of Salvador Dali, cynically observed: "Just pronounce the magic word 'art,' and everything is okay."

Jane Alexander Sponsors Porno Art

Rather than a seasoned administrator, politician, or businessman, Hillary and Bill picked a stage and screen star, Jane Alexander, to courageously lead the liberal forces of diversity in the arts into the homosexually correct new millennium. Alexander's chief credential for this post seems to be her highly acclaimed (by liberals, naturally) role in the Broadway comedy, *The Sisters Rosensweig*.

The real reason why she fits Hillary and Bill's prerequisites for the job, however, is the fact that Alexander is on record as a champion of more and more government money for lewd and salacious antichrist art. Congressman Sidney Yates (D-Ill), chairman of the House Committee that reviews appropriations for the NEA, remembers Ms. Alexander as an outspoken critic of conservative legislators in past sessions of congress attempting to bridle the stridently gay and commuNazi focus of the agency. At a press conference, Rep. Yates admiringly noted that during the Bush era, Jane

Alexander had testified before his panel in support of continued NEA funding of objectionable art projects.[5]

"I was taken by her charm, knowledge, and sincerity," said Yates, himself an advocate of NEA grants for porno-blasphemous works of art. "I think she'll do a great deal to bring prestige to the NEA."[6]

"Prestige?" The fact is that Jane Alexander was chosen because she can be trusted by Hillary to aggressively champion and fund lesbian and homosexual art. That's why I bequeath her the moniker of "The Czarina of Homoerotic Art."

M A Y A
A N G E L O U

Position: Inaugural Poet

Moniker: *Rainbow Earth Mother*

With the Bill Clinton and Al Gore inauguration on January 20, 1993, the people of America quite obviously left the realms of presidential dignity and good taste and entered some kind of bizarre twilight zone of demonic weirdness. How else can you explain the preposterous events that occurred?

During the week of the inaugural festivities, the nation was treated to a gay, lesbian and homosexual band trooping down Pennsylvania Avenue. Then there were the gala parties and balls which the dynamic quadruplet—Bill, Hillary, Al, and Tipper—attended. The performers included Bill's favorite rock band, *Fleetwood Mac*, with self-proclaimed witch, Stevie Nicks, on the vocals. And naturally, there were the Elvis impersonators, Barbara Streisand, and all the other glitzy Hollywood stars. Immersed in ecstasy, the dynamic quadruplet literally drank and danced the nights away.[1]

"New World Order" Remains On Target

Then came the strange but ominous inaugural ceremony. Clinton gave a brief speech in which he mentioned the word "change" eleven times. The new U.S. president also announced that, "There is now no distinction between domestic and foreign policy." Our problems and our responsibilities, said the baby boomer chief executive, are *global*. This was, of course, a signal that the New World Order goal of the elitists remains on target. Clinton ended his globalist sermonette with a reading—I'm not joking!—from Scripture.[2]

Next, Mother Earth religious poet *Maya Angelou* arose to give an original poetry reading. Angelou, a darling of the New Age crowd, wowed an international TV audience with dreamy, spiritually-oriented lyrics which had human beings talking to rocks, trees, forests, and rivers. The poem also stated something to the effect that the Earth and its people "are one."[3]

It was very touching and sensitive—that is, if you're one of those witchcraft, environmentalist, New Age types into crystals, the worship of the Mother Earth goddess, Hindu pantheism, and so forth.

Maya Angelou told *People* magazine that she prepared for the inauguration by checking into a hotel room with only her pen, a writing pad, a bottle of sherry, and a Bible.[4] She related to *U.S.A. Today* that she is a constant churchgoer, adding that it didn't matter *which church* she attends. Angelou proudly explained that she frequents Moslem mosques, Jewish synagogues, Buddhist temples, and pro-gay, Protestant churches with equal enthusiasm.[5]

Demonstrating Against the U.S. Flag

Ms. Angelou was interviewed back in 1990 by *Magical Blend*, a popular New Age magazine.[6] In that interview, she discussed her friendship with the late Malcolm X, the Black Muslim leader who often referred to Caucasians as "white devils." Angelou also reminisced about the time she was in Accra, Ghana, in Africa, participating in a demonstration against the American Embassy. Here is how she described her part in that radical event:

> We in fact were marching against the American Embassy. About just after dawn two soldiers came out of the building and walked with the folded flag to the flagstand, and suddenly, I guess they were nervous ... We started shouting.[7]

Isn't it fascinating that Bill Clinton himself once led anti-American demonstrations overseas against this very same flag—the stars and stripes? Clinton did this first in Oxford, England and then later in communist Russia, in Moscow.[8]

A Strange Prayer, A Stranger Hand Sign

Following poet Maya Angelou's pantheistic Mother Earth stanzas, famed evangelist Billy Graham got up and prayed, asking God's blessings on the president and the country.

As soon as Graham's short prayer of benediction ended, the huge and enthusiastic crowd went wild. Gay men and lesbians were seen warmly embracing their partners, kissing and stroking each other's body parts. At the podium, behind a virtually invisible bulletproof, glass shield, Bill, Hillary, and Chelsea Clinton stood, smiled, and waved to the throng.

Then, suddenly, he did it. Bill Clinton flashed what some say appeared to be the sign of the devil's horns with his left hand. It happened in an instant, but not before the cameras had captured the dramatic scene on film.[9]

All in all, this was a weird extravaganza: a week of witchery, sodomizing, New Age quackery, and satanic symphonies. And culminating it all was an anointing of the chief culprit responsible, the newly elected president of the United States, by the world's most admired clergyman. Yes, this was fantastic, mind-blowing theater of which the late Rod Serling, noted producer of the classic TV series, *The Twilight Zone*, would have been proud.

A Mind-blowing Example

Maya Angelou is, herself, a brilliant example of mind-blowing theater and illusion. A pal of Hillary's hailing from the little town of Stamps, Arkansas, Ms. Angelou's inaugural day performance thrilled the gay, liberal, and New Age communities. This was someone they could relate to, said her fellow poets and strange people everywhere.

"Just having her there, Clinton has reawakened possibilities," said Haki Madhubuti, founder of Third World Press in Chicago, himself a poet. "It was beautiful symbolism," he added. "Angelou's juxtaposing the spiritual with the secular was very important."[10]

Marilyn Millay, a reporter from *Newsday*, gushed with unreserved acclaim for the "diversity" contained in Angelou's poetry. "Angelou's poem," wrote Millay, "was a catalog of U.S. diversity with references to Asians, Hispanics, Jews, Africans, Native Americans, Catholics, Muslims, and the Irish," as well as "the gay, the straight, the preacher, the privileged, the homeless, the teacher."[11]

"Really, it was a manifesto, a meditation, a blessing . . . It was a very spiritual piece," said Marita Golden, a writer and professor of English at George Mason University in Virginia.[12]

Yes, the liberals cooed and swooned over Maya's pantheistic, unity-in-diversity bit of confused and garbled eco-babble poetry. It was only natural that they would. After all, here was a 64-year old black woman quoting a talking

Rock, a talking River, and a talking Tree, each of which called out to "the Priest, the Sheikh, the Sioux, the Jew, the French," and so on. Indeed, in her inaugural poem, everyone but the *Christian* and the *American patriot* were mentioned by Angelou's living, talking earth "beings"—the Rock, the River, and the Tree.[13]

Isn't it curious that the Muslim, the Jew, and so forth were specifically called out to be a part of Maya Angelou's "new world," her new horizon, but the term "Christian" seemed to be purposefully omitted? Meanwhile, ethnic group after ethnic group was mentioned, but no recognition given to a melting pot America nor to any patriotic symbols.

Naturally, Hillary's chosen poet, Maya Angelou, did talk about the pollution of the environment in her universally acclaimed (by liberals, Eastern religionists and New Agers) inaugural poem. She mouthed words by "Mother Earth," accusing the profit-mongers of casting "currents of debris upon my breast."[14]

Yes, good old Mother Earth, the New Age's grand deity, was given her due by Maya. But having closely examined the written transcript of her inaugural poem, entitled "On the Pulse of Morning," I could find no reference to Jesus, to the Bible, or to the traditional tenets of the Christian faith.

This is understandable, however, once we begin to delve into the embarrassingly ragged life and times of this woman, Maya Angelou, chosen especially by Hillary and Bill Clinton to be the first poet since the famed Robert Frost to recite a poem at a presidential inauguration. Remember, this woman and her poetry were picked for exaltation and deification by the Clintons for a purpose. *Maya Angelou is Hillary and Bill's role model for the 21st century, New Age female.*

A Prostitute and Stripper—and Baptist University Professor!

The *American Information Newsletter* published a most revealing article about Maya Angelou in its May 1993 edition.

I'm reprinting this article below because of its implications for our understanding of *why* and *how* Maya Angelou, a former prostitute, stripper and anti-U.S.A. flag demonstrator, was chosen by the Clintons to exemplify their vision for the New World to come:

Critic Of Black Inaugural Poet Sued By University

The black poetess who gave a reading at the Clinton inaugural and whose poem was treated as nearly holy by the socio-fascist media, came under fire by a conservative student editor at the university at which she has a position.

Maya Angelou (born Margaret Johnson) read her poem "Rock, River, Tree" at the Clinton celebration. Shortly after editor John Meroney of the *Wake Forest Critic*—an independent student publication at Wake Forest University—published an exposé on Angelou/Johnson, he received a letter from university lawyers demanding the publication drop "Wake Forest" from its name.

The university claims the legal threat has nothing to do with the Meroney article on Angelou/Johnson which appeared in the national publication, *The American Spectator*. It appeared under Meroney's byline as the editor of the *Wake Forest Critic*. Meroney disagrees. He said, "the university didn't like these things being exposed . . . It's a clear attempt by the administration to close the paper down."

Meroney charged that the new favorite of the socio-fascist press since the Clinton bash is in fact a former prostitute and stripper whose favorite poetic subjects are life as a single mother, life in Berkeley and her alleged rape at age seven.

Meroney also questions if Angelou/Johnson, who says she does not regret her life as a prostitute and stripper, is a

Christian. Wake Forest is a Southern Baptist university and Angelou/Johnson claims to be a church member but Meroney says he has never heard her tell of a conversion or show repentance for her past sinful life.

Wake Forest responded to the Meroney revelations about the poetess' limited work load by describing Angelou/ Johnson as essentially an affirmative action appointee. A university spokesman said, "she has been a leader in helping Wake Forest University meet its moral obligation to diversify our student body and faculty."[15]

In his *American Spectator* article, entitled "The Real Maya Angelou," John Meroney also noted that Maya Angelou "has gained attention as a columnist for *Playgirl*," the vulgar, female imitation of Hugh Hefner's *Playboy* magazine. "She describes herself in interviews and books," Meroney says, "as a former Madam, prostitute, burlesque stripper, and advisor to Malcolm X."[16]

What is really perverse is that Angelou has been appointed "Professor for Life" by a *Southern Baptist university—Wake Forest!* She's paid over $100,000 a year, yet the university's leaders require no work of her! At one time, Angelou claimed she "might" teach a course on the "Philosophy of Liberation," but that never transpired. Meroney writes:

She collects an annual salary well into the six figures, yet presently teaches no classes and has no campus office. The office listed for her in the Wake Forest University telephone directory is a storage closet. Her phone number gives an electronic voice mail recording that announces only the extension number; calls to it are not returned.[17]

Referring to Clinton's choice of Maya Angelou to perform at the inaugural event, Meroney wryly comments, "Clinton gave us a phantom professor with a broom-closet office and an assumed name."[18]

A New Religion for a Liberal Age

Maya Angelou's given first name, as noted above, was Margaret, and her last name was "Johnson" or "Macdonald," depending on the version told by she and her friends. Why "Maya" and why "Angelou?" *Maya* is a name for the Hindu goddess who, according to that Eastern religion, created the universe. It is also a Hindu word meaning "illusion."[19] Margaret obviously considers herself an angel (Angelou) or goddess of illusion!

How becoming a name for the premier poet of a new liberal age! Not surprisingly, the teachings of the Hindu goddess and the pantheistic, New Age religion are closely allied with witchcraft (or *Wicca*), which also is implicitly found in the works of Hillary's poet laureate, Maya Angelou. Such teachings, regrettably, are finding increasing merit among liberals everywhere. Many an atheist or lukewarm Christian has also embraced the new earth and rainbow religion of pageantry and illusion.

Is Maya Angelou a Porno Writer?

Maya Angelou has received numerous awards for her writing, mostly from the liberal "Illaterati" who are always quick to applaud writers, playwrights, and other authors who birth hyper-feminist and pseudo-pornographic trash. Wanting to familiarize myself with Maya's literary works. I went to a local bookstore and found a copy of her book, *Now Sheba Sings The Song*, illustrated with "art" by Tom Feelings, one of Maya's friends from her anti-U.S. demonstration days back in Ghana, Africa.[20]

I expected the book to be bad, but not *this bad!* The title page, just inside the front cover, got my immediate, rapt attention. I winced because I recognized this drawing for what I believe it is: a depiction of a demonically possessed, witch goddess worshipper paying homage to the lunar deity. Inside, the drawings weren't much better. On one page was a drawing of a nude, black woman sprawled on her back, her breasts and genital area vividly displayed. For some this may be art. To me, it is crass, crude pornography posing as art.

On the acknowledgements page, author Maya Angelou dedicated her book "To all my black, brown, beige, yellow, red, and white sisters." (Noteworthy perhaps is the fact that her "white sisters" were mentioned last).[21] Throughout the volume can be found drawings of African and other black women accompanied by examples of her poetic styled prose.

"My breasts are the fullness of mangos in a royal forest, constant, swaying, jungle flowers," Angelou pens on page 29 of *Now Sheba Sings The Song.*[22]

"My impertinent buttocks (high, redolent, tight as dark drums) introduce frenzy into the hearts of small men," she writes on page 33.[23]

On succeeding pages Maya Angelou speaks of "the lusts and leers" of her lover and of the "delicious occasion" when her lover takes her.[24]

Finally, on page 54, in a classic and gritty, pagan religious style which extolls pantheistic doctrines of old, Ms. Angelou speaks as if women exemplify the Earth Mother herself: "I am mate to Kilimanjaro Fujiyama, Mont Blanc and Sister to Everest. He who is daring and brave will know what to do."[25]

The Rainbow Earth Religion

In both the writings in this book and in her inaugural poem, Maya Angelou provides convincing documentation that hers is not the traditional form of Christianity. Her creator is the Cosmos and Earth, not a heavenly Father. Like Al Gore and other environmental spiritualists, "God" is found solely in the whole—in the interconnectedness of all that is. Man, woman, animals, trees, rocks, gemstones, rivers, the stars—all are "God."

True religion, according to the Earth Religion, is to serve Gaia, our Mother the Globe, and to consider sacred and divine all of creation (except for unborn babies, of course). Patriarchal, straight society is said to be evil and dysfunctional. The male-dominated Christian churches are thought to be in dire need of feminization.

Only the religions which deny exclusivity are appropriate to Earth religionists. Biblical Christians, because they refuse to pray to "our Mother which art in heaven" and doggedly insist that Jesus Christ is who He claimed to be—*the* way, *the* truth, *the* life—are to be sneered at, looked down on, and discriminated against. Such are separatists who constitute, in the warped and distorted minds of the devotee's of Mother Earth, a significant threat to the harmony and unity of all other sects, cults, and religions, and to the Earth herself.

As if to emphasize and underscore her disdain for the Christian way of life and her distaste for traditional American values, Maya Angelou is active in the bigoted, Christian-bashing organization, *People For The American Way (PAW)*. Angelou is a member of PAW's board of directors for the state of North Carolina.[26] Led by TV producer Norman Lear *(All in the Family)*, PAW works nonstop to denounce the "Religious Right." The group especially attempts to counter the efforts of Christian parents to remove pornographic and New Age materials from public school classrooms.

It figures that Norman Lear, PAW's founder, is a close friend of the Clintons and is a frequent guest of theirs at the White House. And thus, we can understand why Maya Angelou was Hillary's personal choice to recite poetry on what was undoubtedly the most momentous and important day of her and her husband, Bill's, lives. Well over a billion people around the globe viewed the presidential inauguration. What a pulpit for the New Age religious philosophy! Surely, Hillary did a number on Christianity and on the American people that deceitful day, January 20, 1993, when Maya Angelou, former stripper, prostitute, racial agitator, socialist, anti-American flag demonstrator, and unqualified Wake Forest professor, stood to her feet and read her unholy pagan propaganda piece in poetry.

The National Religious Broadcasters and Maya Angelou

Strangely, support for Maya Angelou's new earth religion can even be found within the evangelical Christian community. On February 14, 1993, Angela Lansbury, the popular Hollywood stage and TV actress *(Murder, She Wrote)* was a keynote speaker for the international convention of the National Religious Broadcasters (NRB), an industry group made up of top-name TV and radio evangelists. In her presentation, Lansbury raved about the wonderful religious philosophy found in Maya Angelou's inaugural poetry. Since the NRB, until recent years, was considered a conservative Christian organization, this provides graphic and alarming evidence that the Christian establishment has strayed far from the truth and has become dangerously corrupted.

The moral collapse of the National Religious Broadcasters has been noted by a small but influential group of high integrity Christian broadcasters who have united to bring reform and revival to Christian TV and radio ministry. Calling itself *Broadcasters United for Revival and Reformation (BURR)*, and headquartered in Milwaukee (address: P.O. Box 08385, Milwaukee, Wisconsin 53208), BURR is led by Ingrid Guzman, of Wisconsin Youth for Christ and co-host of *Crosstalk*, a daily Christian talk show heard across the U.S.A.

The day after the NRB's 1993 convention, BURR issued this press release concerning Angela Lansbury's endorsement at the NRB of Hillary's friend, Maya Angelou:

> Broadcasters United for Revival and Reformation expresses deep concern about the content of Angela Lansbury's address on Hollywood Night, Sunday, February 14 at the 1993 NRB Convention.
>
> After the audience viewed a video collage of some of her work, NRB convention attendees gave her an ovation that lasted several minutes. Noticeably absent from the video collage were the numerous "bad girl" roles she became

famous for, including her role as a Madam of a whorehouse in the 1949 movie, "The Harvey Girls." Also missing were scenes from her upcoming role as a prostitute on the CBS series, "Murder, She Wrote." (The Star 1/26/93)

In her address to the convention, Angela Lansbury not only failed to mention Jesus Christ, she quoted from well known New-Age poetess Maya Angelou, reciting some of the lines that Ms. Angelou read recently at the Clinton inauguration. Sternly, she reminded those present that our nation is comprised of Buddhists, Native Americans and yes, gays. Tolerance and diversity, according to Ms. Lansbury, are the pressing issues of the day for religious broadcasters. Ms. Lansbury concluded her remarks by referring to the "oneness" she feels with God.

In attendance on Sunday night was author and speaker on the New Age, Gary Kah. "There is no question that the tone and message that came across smacked of the New Age Movement," said Kah. "I was stunned to hear something like this at an NRB convention."

NRB Convention attendee and B.U.R.R. Board Member, D. Gregory Mueller was equally concerned. "What was coming from Angela Lansbury was really the same thing we are hearing from Hollywood as a whole: diversity and tolerance must be upheld, even if the lifestyle in question is an abomination to the Lord."

Hollywood Night at this NRB Convention has again underscored the clear need for a *new generation* of young Christian broadcasters to rise up and be heard; young people who aren't afraid to challenge the status quo and address spiritual compromise head on. The time for feel good, celebrity worshipping evangelicalism in Christian broadcasting is long gone. The darkness is deepening and we *must* seek God's face.[27]

CAROL BELLAMY

Position: Director of the
Peace Corps

Moniker: *Molly Ivins' Friend*

Ms. Bellamy is a bonafide liberal who's long been tied in to Hillary's femiNazi network. Bellamy, the former City Council President in New York, was one of President Clinton's earliest New York supporters. She's known Hillary for years and is also bosom buddies with several other of Hillary's Hellcats.[1]

According to *The Washington Post*, Carol Bellamy is very close friends with Donna Shalala, Hillary's choice as Secretary of Health and Human Services.[2] The *Post* also reported that Shalala, Bellamy, and a mutual pal, nationally syndicated, newspaper columnist Molly Ivins, love to take "exotic vacations" together. Molly Ivins, author of the anti-conservative smear book, *Molly Ivins Can't Say That, Can She?*, is a Dallas, Texas resident whose ultra-liberal newspaper columns have drawn the ire of moderates and conservatives alike. Ivin's writings indicate that she is especially fond of bashing biblical Christians. She once referred to conservative-oriented, Southern Baptist pastors as "Shiite Baptists," thus comparing them to Ayatallah Khomeini's radical Islamic mullahs.

C A R O L
B R O W N E R

Position: Head of the Environmental
Protection Agency

Moniker: *The Land Grabber*

Carol Browner is the new boss woman of the Environmental
Protection Agency (EPA), the agency that specializes in
harassing land owners everywhere and delights in putting
tens of thousands of forest workers on unemployment lines.
As we shall see, Ms. Browner perfectly fits the mold of one
of Hillary's women.

First, we find that *Browner* is Carol's maiden name, not
her husband's last name. This is just what Hillary Rodham
did in the pre-cookies days before her husband Bill hit the
campaign trail. Ms. Browner is married to a hapless gent
named *Mr. Podhorzer*. Carol refused to go along with changing
her name on their wedding day, just as feminist Hillary
Rodham at first refused to accept the Clinton tag and even
now insists on being called Hillary Rodham Clinton.[1]

Second, we note that Carol Podhorzer (*aka* Carol Browner)
is, like her friend Hillary, a lawyer—a *very rich* lawyer.
She's also a seasoned politician. She first worked for Senator
Lawton Chiles (D-FL) and then for Senator (now VP) Al
"Spotted Owl" Gore, whose absurdly preposterous,
environmental philosophy mirrors that of Browner's. It should
because, reportedly, it was Carol Browner who was the
ghost writer for Al Gore's eco-babble, bestseller book, *Earth
in the Balance*.

In her/his book, Ms. Browner calls for a "Global Marshall
Plan," in which U.S. taxpayers will foot the bill to a tune of
at least $100 billion to clean up the pollution in Third World
countries such as Mexico. In fact, President Clinton's
outrageous proposal for the North American Free Trade Act
(NAFTA) provides for Americans to spend billions to clean

up corporate filth inside Mexico along the Texas and California borders.

Browner, NAFTA, and Eco-Nonsense

Here, essentially, is the plan: first, NAFTA will put millions of Americans out of work by encouraging U.S.-based companies to move their manufacturing operations to Mexico, where labor can be had dirt cheap, thus abandoning the already crippled U.S. economy.

Then, when these same new plants and factories have taken full advantage of Mexico's lax—virtually nonexistent—environmental laws, dirtied the environment and filled it with dangerous chemicals and toxins, the impoverished U.S. taxpayers are expected to step in, open their pocketbooks for the umpteenth time, and clean up the mess. We are to become Mexico's janitors and sanitary squad.

That's the Rockefeller-sponsored, New World Order, capitalist, global economy: the super rich *play*, the everyday, bankrupt American citizen *pays*.

In their book, Browner and Gore constantly refer to the most faulty and ridiculous pseudo-scientific "studies"—usually studies conducted by uneducated, New Age eco-fanatics to support their wacky environmental religion. Contrary to these flawed environmental treatises, statistics published by the National Weather Service, NASA, and other scientific agencies consistently report that the earth has actually gotten slightly *cooler* during the past decade. Yet, the Browner/ Gore, Mother Earth spiritualists are like chicken littles, running around exclaiming, "The earth is warming, the earth is warming!"

Other scare tactics by the environmental extremists are similarly flawed and not based on scientific facts. For example, regardless of eco-propaganda, there is no severe or extraordinary *ozone* depletion in the atmosphere other than due to cyclical, self-correcting factors. CFCs do *not* cause ozone depletion. This in spite of the fact that relatively inexpensive freon is going to be banned by the environuts, driving up the costs of home and auto air conditioners by hundreds, perhaps thousands, of dollars per unit.[2]

They Want to Control Us

No, there is *no* scientific justification for what the Hillbillary administration and Ms. Browner want to do to us concerning the environment. So *what is* the reason for their draconian proposals? The answer, once again, is simple: *control.* The environmental "crisis" gives the One Worlders a fabulous opportunity to control all of us. Consider these disturbing facts:

❑ Zillions of pages of regulations now minutely tell businesses, home owners, and land owners what they can and can't do with their own land. *Score one for the envirobureaucrats.*

❑ Billions of dollars are annually extracted from taxpayers' salaries, wages, earnings, and capital gains, to be squandered on questionable "Save the Earth" projects. That's robbing the taxpayers and controlling them through IRS red tape. *Score two for the envirobureaucrats.*

❑ The Christian Church is continually lambasted by the Gore/Browner/Clinton faction. Christians are scorned for their "Armageddon mentality." Because they emphasize the gospel message and the spirituality of man rather than worshipping divine "Mother Earth," Christians are branded a threat to the environment. Gore and Browner, in their pagan, New Age book, *Earth in the Balance,* ridiculously contend that such favored religions as the revived Goddess Movement, Buddhism, Hinduism, and Native American Indian animism and "Great Spirit" worship are "earth honoring," while Biblical Christianity is not. *Score three for the envirobureaucrats.*

With the score now "three to zip," the globalist propagandists are successfully pushing for implementation of their *hidden agenda*. Their scheme calls for an intrusive United Nations bureaucracy, guided behind the scenes by a Secret Brotherhood of controllers, to be given worldwide, dictatorial powers. This bureaucracy, having police enforcement powers, will operate across national boundaries. To obtain this maximum control, the people have to be conned into believing that such a drastic, totalitarian solution is vital and necessary to solve the (contrived) crisis.

This was the reason for the Earth Summit in Rio de Janeiro in the summer of 1992, which Al Gore dutifully attended, making a fool of himself with his silly preaching of the new, unscientific, Mother Earth, environmental religion. Behind closed doors in Rio, the elite mapped out their plans to continue their massive public relations campaign to reeducate and reorient the mass mind. They also set up machinery, including a World Conservation Bank, to enable them to be paid by U.S. taxpayers to grab title to millions of acres of resource-rich wilderness lands around the globe, including in the U.S.A.

The fact is that the environmental scam affords the super rich conspirators the best opportunities to control the American people and establish the New World Order. Previously, war and armed conflict were deemed necessary for the elitists to gain ground. But their experience in setting up and funding thousands of activist *front groups* posing as citizen-led, environmental organizations, has convinced the elite that it is wisest, safer, and more efficient to use the environmental stratagem to gain control of nations and peoples.

After all, war leaves in its wake economic devastation and the ruination of many financial resources owned by the elitists. The environmental stratagem, on the other hand, for the most part leaves factories, real estate, and other tangibles and economic structures intact.

The Land Grabbers

As chief of the nation's top environmental bureaucracy, Carol Browner (*aka* Podhorzer) possesses the brute, administrative police power that will be required to topple resistance to the fast-emerging, pseudo-democratic world dictatorship. Wielding a blinding array of regulations and codes available at the EPA, she and Hillary have full authority to harass and intimidate small businesses, to confiscate and take land (in violation of the U.S. Constitution's clear requirement that the *eminent domain* principle be used so that property owners be financially compensated for "takings" by government), and close down businesses that do not conform to the ecological *Prime Directive* of the elite controllers.

This is the socio-fascist plot of the Clintonistas: to steal people's land from them, claiming all the while that they're only doing it to protect the "diversity" of Mother Earth. Audubon Society President Peter Berline has said: "We reject the idea of property rights . . . We reject the Constitution giving unbridled rights to property owners."[3]

In his outstanding publication, *The Intelligence Advisor*, Don McAlvany writes:

> Using environmentalism for political cover, liberal (fascist) bureaucrats are rendering millions of acres of land across America useless and obliterating the property rights of thousands of landowners. The 1990 Federal Register lists more than 63,000 (that's right 63,000) new regulations restricting the use of private property.[4]

The key, of course, is to keep in mind that the super rich, the Clintonistas, the Rockefeller elite, will not be required to give up *their* property rights. The Federal Reserve banks are secure. It is the little people, so-called, the everyday American man and woman, who has made this country great— yes, it is *we the people* who are being robbed of our land and stripped of our constitutional rights.

Environmentalism and the New Fascist State

It is no accident that Hitler was an avid environmentalist who sought to cleanse and purify the earth of people in a vain and foolhardy attempt to provide *Lebensraum* (living room) for his superior race. The Nazis were "green," and Hitler and his jackboot followers were vegetarians and holistic health food nuts. They worshipped the sacred earth and they despised perishable, inferior man. The Hitlerians believed that both nature and the superior, New Age Superman were interconnected. They believed in the interconnectedness of all things.

Those who, like Browner, Gore, and the Clintons, would make nature a god and reintroduce paganism to society must, eventually, logically arrive at the same conclusion as the Nazis and fascists: that the *state*, or as they call it, *community*, should be worshipped. Philosophically, the deified state, organized by an elite, is nature. Theirs is a closed system of mutual, though stagnant, protection. What they see as the interconnectedness between animals (including humans), insects, birds, and all of the cosmos is a putrefying, closed system. In such a closed and decaying system, the *community* is exalted and made sacrosanct; whereas the *individual person* is debased and diminished.

Is this why Hillary and Bill have no compunction against using deceit and trickery to win high office, and then, once elected, go on to break campaign promise after campaign promise? Hillary's new "Politics of Meaning" and her statement that we need to "redefine what it means to be a human" indicate that she has little respect for the individual human dignity afforded men and women by God and set forth in the Holy Bible.

In the New Age philosophy, sharpened for the Clintons at places like Hilton Head, South Carolina, where the Clintons spent much time at "Renaissance" weekends, the "community" (Communism and Nazism called it the "state") is to be the principle unit of focus and emphasis. Collective salvation is the way the New World Order is to be implemented. The age of the individual, or *homo sapien,* is at an end, say the New Order advocates. The age of *homo noeticus*—the "New Man," a super being inextricably tied to and interconnected with his/her fellow animals and the earth—is at hand.

Without an understanding of the hideous, underlying Luciferian *spiritual nature* of the Hillbillary administration's environmental policies and objectives, we cannot adequately fight back and win. And win we must, if principled, individual man, separate from and yet a good steward of the earth, under the sovereignty of and responsible to God, is not to perish from the earth.

D R .   J O Y C E L Y N   E L D E R S

Position: Surgeon General of the United States

Moniker: *The Condom Queen*

"We've taught our children in driver's education what to do in the front seat, and now we've got to teach them what to do in the back seat." —Surgeon General Joycelyn Elders, speaking to the Association of Reproductive Health Professionals Conference (January 31, 1993)

"Newsflash! A condom queen becomes the guardian of America's health." That's what the newspaper headlines should have said when Dr. Joycelyn Elders was named Surgeon General. But they didn't, because Dr. Joycelyn Elders is the darling of the liberal media and, therefore, is protected by her think-mates in the press.

As far as Elders is concerned, condoms are the answer to everything, maybe even the conflict in Bosnia. Sexual promiscuity isn't a problem, Dr. Joycelyn Elders insists; it's okay for even the youngest of kids to "do it." The problem, she says, is being protected by a condom *when* you do it.

Elders is a physician who has a lot of unusual ideas about sex, birth controls, abortion, and even slavery. To the majority of Americans who profess a strong belief in traditional values, the bizarre views expressed by Elders may just as well have come from an alien from the planet Venus. Unfortunately for this nation, these insane absurdities come not only from a trained medical doctor, they come from a radical-thinking woman whom Hillary and Bill have made our Surgeon General of the United States of America!

A Wild Woman Consumed by Sex

To say that Joycelyn Elders is a wild woman *consumed* by thoughts of sex is not an understatement. She's absolutely fascinated with the subject. Other serious health and social issues—ranging from diseases and illnesses such as cancer and heart disease to such ills as tobacco smoking and alcoholism—pale in significance. To Elders, the *one* major issue of our day is to encourage "safe sex"—and the more of it the better.

Insiders who know Joycelyn Elders explain that her obsessive preoccupation with the subject of sex is made apparent in almost every facet of her life and work. Matt Friedman, writing in the *Clarion-Ledger*, a daily newspaper out of Jackson, Mississippi, notes that some visitors to Elders' own office have been shocked to discover a weird contraption sitting in plain view right on top of her desk. Proudly, a smiling and talkative Dr. Elders tells her bemused, and sometimes offended, guests that this is an "Ozark Rubber Tree"—so called because yellow condoms hang down from its stalks.[1]

Yellow condoms?

Attached to Elders' Ozark Rubber Tree is an off-color note blatantly and directly referring to male erection and sexual activity: "Blooms mostly at night. Blooms vary in length, depending on owner. Blooms may wilt in chilly atmosphere."[2]

As if this vulgar display of sexual buffoonery wasn't enough to cause alarm and disbelief in the minds of unsuspecting victims who come to visit her, Elders' own unique brand of social and moral (or should we say, "immoral?") philosophies, that she spouts to anyone unfortunate enough to be in listening range, provide the icing on the cake. To anyone who will listen, she shoots her mouth off. She wants the nation to institute explicit, no holds barred sex education beginning with every kindergartner, says Elders, and she's not going to let a bunch of traditional Americans and a "male-dominated clergy" stand in the way of her agenda for the whole nation.[3]

Abortion Instruction for Pre-Schoolers?

Interviewed on television about her plan to teach pre-schoolers how to have plenty of fun through "safe sex" experiences, the indefatigable Dr. Elders gushed about the concept. "We've got to have *"abor . . . ,"* I mean, *contraception,* taught at the earliest levels of education," she explained.[4]

Her slip of the word "abor . . ." (abortion) reveals that what Elders really has in mind is the propagandizing and indoctrination of the youngest of children on the "merits" of abortion. Instantly realizing—even as she spoke and began to utter the "A" word—that this idea would no doubt receive a frosty reception from most viewers and would let the "cat out of the bag" as to her ultimate intentions, Elders quickly inserted the safer, undefined and more nebulous term, "contraception."

The majority of Americans would be shocked to even imagine a mandatory public school program which has adult teachers instructing 3 and 4-year olds on how to put on and wear a condom! But Dr. Elders is not embarrassed one wit that most Americans find her ideas on sex education for the youngest of kids abhorrent and perverted. "Give me the choice of trying to educate a 3-year old or trying to educate an 18-year old, and I'll take the 3-year old every time," she has stated.[5]

The very thought of interrupting the education of 3, 4, and 5-year olds and polluting their tender young minds with images of condom usage and various modes of sexual conduct is disgusting and perverse to most Americans. But liberals like Joycelyn Elders and Hillary Clinton just don't understand the big taboo here. "Sexuality education beginning in education" should be our goal, Elders told the *Arkansas Gazette* in 1988.[6]

Of course, Elders doesn't think that sex counseling and psychotherapy should stop with just the dayschool set. She also wants every well-dressed teenage girl to think of the condom as a necessary component in a well-stocked purse— much like a tube of lipstick or a comb. "I tell every girl," the crazed, pro-sex doctor once declared on national television, "that when she goes out on a date, put a condom in her purse."[7]

Parents Too Stupid to be Consulted

The fact that parents might find this both offensive and a violation of family privacy does not deter the woman who has disparagingly been called the "Condom Queen" and has also been labeled by her conservative critics as the "Czarina of Outrageous Statements." Elders arrogantly rattles the line that parents should not be given a choice in the matter. After all, she adds, most parents are too stupid and dumb to handle the task of sex education at home. So the "sex expert" teachers of our kindergarteners, she insists, must be empowered to do the job.[8]

"Some people say parents should educate children about health care and sex education," Elders told the Conway Arkansas *Log Cabin Democrat* in 1991, "but many parents are uneducated."[9]

Neither can parents be entrusted with condom distribution

to kids, either, Elders explains. That's why she favors school-based health clinics be set up in public schools throughout America. The clinics will be manned, of course, by "health reproductive specialists": pro-abortion activists trained to parrot to kids propaganda about the advantages of safe sex and readily available abortion services.

At such school-based clinics, free condoms for teenagers are passed out at taxpayers' expense. But what if the condoms fail and pregnancy occurs? Then, says Elders, abortions must be provided to all who can be persuaded to have them. In such cases, parents need not be notified. Their approval—or disapproval—she says, is quite irrelevant. In the Hillary Clinton-Joycelyn Elders school of social engineering, the curriculum demands that children's rights be strictly adhered to, but family and parents' rights are nonexistent.

Although there are fewer than 200 school-based health clinics in the thousands of public schools across the U.S.A., the tiny state of Arkansas has 24 such clinics in only 11 counties. All were established under the watchful eye and exuberant, pro-sex spirit of Joycelyn Elders. Each clinic costs about $150,000 annually to operate.[10]

When the citizens of Arkansas first found out that these clinics were not there to handle sprained ankles and upset stomachs, but to dispense condoms and promote sexual promiscuity through "affirmative" counseling, an uproar of dissent ensued. Many parents refused to return consent forms to their local schools. Elders simply told the health clinics to "assume" that the parents are giving consent. Abortions also were arranged without parental notification.[11]

The Breeding of Slaves and Prostitutes

As Surgeon General, Elders advocates the termination of out-of-wedlock teen pregnancies by abortion for reason of economic convenience. Children who have children become society's "slaves," says Elders. Unmarried, pregnant, teenage girls, she insultingly reports, "are breeding another class of slaves at a time when we don't need any more slaves."[12]

Condoms, however, are not enough, Elders reports. Far better than condoms, she says, is to require sexually active, teenage girls to be fitted with *Norplant*, the subcutaneously applied (under the skin) pharmaceutical contraceptive.[13]

Although Joycelyn Elders is, herself, a black American, she, Hillary, and their liberal friends seem to be especially fascinated about providing the $500 per unit Norplant implant to black teenagers from ghetto and slum neighborhoods in decaying urban centers where pregnancy rates are now soaring. Naturally, taxpayers will be required to foot the bill.

Liberal activists bristle with righteous indignation at the suggestion by thoughtful conservatives that this might just be an example of racism, since it is African-American, rather than white girls, who are targeted for implants and other preventive measures. Is this just a racist ploy to reduce the black population? "Nah," respond the radical women in charge of the nation's contraceptive health policies. And anyone who even broaches the subject, they acidly add, is an intolerant bigot!

According to Dr. Elders, teens are not to be the only segment of the population to be given Norplant at taxpayer expense, either. Drug-addicted prostitutes, too, would be given the contraceptive implant to prevent babies being conceived.

During a guest appearance on the *Talk Live* national radio program hosted by radical, pro-abortion activist Faye Wattleton, formerly the president of Planned Parenthood, Elders was asked about this possibility. Her reply indicates that she is not as dismayed by the brutal and tragic, life-destroying reality of prostitution and drug abuse as she is excited over the "opportunity" to prevent unwanted births.

"I would hope that we would be able to provide them (prostitutes) with Norplant," Dr. Elders remarked, "so they could still use sex if they must to buy their drugs and not have unplanned babies."[14]

Defective Condoms, Courtesy of Dr. Joycelyn Elders

The nation's top doctor, our Surgeon General, is, in fact, so enamored of contraceptives and birth control devices that, as Governor Clinton's cabinet-level, health officer for the state of Arkansas, she once ordered the distribution to teenagers in public schools of *defective* condoms. She was informed by subordinates that a study had found that a small, though significant, percentage of the condoms purchased by the state for its schools were defective and, therefore, ineffective in preventing either pregnancies or transmittable diseases (such as AIDS!). One high school clinic, Elders was told, was forced to send back 50 condoms following complaints about them breaking. [15]

Dr. Elders decided to sit on this alarming information and do nothing. To make matters worse, tragically demonstrating her insensitivity and callous disregard for the health and safety of the teens to be given the defective condoms, Elders deceitfully gave instructions that *no warnings or cautionary notice* be provided to recipients and users who were at risk because of the unsafe condoms.

When it was discovered that Elders' state health agency was taking no action to correct the disastrous situation, the federal government obtained a court order to seize the poor quality condoms. The Federal Food and Drug Administration had found a defective rate ten times higher than the limit set by the national standards and was not inclined to cover up the problem.[16]

The Cure for Teen Pregnancies

In 1987, at the time of her appointment as Bill Clinton's health chieftain for Arkansas, Joycelyn Elders announced a grandiose goal. She promised the citizens of the Razorback State that, through generous distribution of condoms and with the "benefits" of accelerated sex education curricula in the schools, Arkansas would be able to cut the teenage pregnancy rate in half while keeping children and teens free of AIDS and other sexually transmitted diseases. Yes, she assured state legislators and critics alike, easy condom availability and sex instruction would be the panacea for these pressing social problems.

Her assertion that providing contraceptive devices to teens and boosting education efforts would reduce teen pregnancies, while guaranteeing "safe sex," is a commonly held assumption among liberals who oppose traditional moral values. To these radical, true believers, "Just say no!"— *sexual abstinence*—is never the answer. Abstinence is not a viable option, they say, because kids are going to have sex anyway. So condoms are the only available alternative, the claim goes, to protect the school-age population from the ravages of disease and the growing plague of unwanted babies.

However, research statistics conclusively prove that, paradoxically, teen pregnancies actually *increase* when sex education curricula are introduced. The same statistics show that pregnancies also rise dramatically when condoms are freely distributed in schools.

The reasons for this seeming anomaly are twofold. First, current sex education teaching strategies employ *relativist ethics* and *values clarification* methodologies. This reinforces the questionable and dubious social philosophy that there are no moral absolutes—every young person has the right to determine his or her own lifestyle choices. Free sex, or premarital sex, is neither discouraged nor depicted as an unacceptable practice but is, instead, proposed to be a *private, pro-choice matter.*

Moreover, students are cautioned by sex education instructors that parents, being old-fashioned and out of touch, are not suitable to be their advisors on sex or other lifestyle choices.

Without a workable moral compass and being deprived of worthwhile, moral guidelines, children are most likely to do "whatever feels good." Sex feels good, so . . . they do it. Sadly, since the emotional maturity of many teenagers is so undeveloped, a boy and girl on a date, who get into a heavy petting situation but discover they are fresh out of a condom, are very likely to go right ahead and have intercourse without any so-called "protection."

Why not? Who's to say they shouldn't? Certainly not their outmoded and "uncool" parents! Anyway, MTV, with its sexually explicit videos; rap music with its lewd, high-charged sexual lyrics; and today's TV situation comedies, movies and other programs, with their unrestricted sexual scenarios and ultra-liberal ideologies, send a message to kids that sexual promiscuity is not only a possibility—it's vastly desirable and cool.

A second reason why sex education fails is that the instruction itself arouses latent sexual feelings within the psyches of immature, fascinated, and impressionable youth. Whether suggestive or explicit, the effects of viewing an erotically stimulating instructional film or discussing actual sexual acts in a class composed of members of the opposite sex can be explosive, energizing youthful hormones and dangerously unleashing pent-up feelings, thoughts, and desires.

Dr. Elders' Programs are Shocking Failures

For dynamic proof that enhancing condom availability and adding more sex education course hours to the curricula is dangerously counterproductive, one has only to examine what happened in the state of Arkansas during Dr. Joycelyn Elders' tenure as director of the Department of Health. According to the U.S. Department of Health and Human Services, Arkansas's teenage birthrate jumped from fourth to second in the nation while Elders was in office. The Arkansas Department of Health reported a dramatic *130 percent rise* in the number of teenagers contracting syphilis. Statistics also showed an alarming *150 percent rise* in teenagers affected with the AIDS HIV virus.[17]

Amazingly, prior to Dr. Joycelyn Elders taking over the state's top health slot, the teen pregnancy rate *had declined* for the five consecutive years between 1980 and 1985. She took a rapidly improving situation and promptly torpedoed it, sinking the schools of the state of Arkansas into a pit of unhealthy moral degeneracy with her so-called "health clinics."[18]

What's more, her campaign to promote safe sex was not only immoral, irresponsible, and a monumental social failure, it also was unbearably expensive. When Arkansas taxpayers balked at giving the Clintons and their fascist doctor more money to set up and run their school-based sex clinics, Hillary, Bill and Joycelyn just reached deeper into the federal government's bulging bag of financial, socialist goodies. According to the *Wall Street Journal*, the Clintons and Elders increased the state's Health Department funding from $67 million in 1987 to a whopping $150 million in 1993, largely through federal funding programs.[19]

In her U.S. Senate confirmation hearings, Dr. Elders, attempting to sugarcoat the concerns of legislators, confessed that she "wasn't proud" of her dismal record in Arkansas, but she went on to speciously claim that if it had not been for her "reproductive health" programs, the statistics would have been even worse.

In an effort to defuse her critics and detractors, which included such powerful, conservative, pro-family groups as Concerned Women for America, The American Family Association, Eagle Forum, the Family Research Council, the Christian Coalition, and the Traditional Values Coalition, Elders also insisted during the hearings that, of course, she herself preferred a policy of sexual abstinence. But, she assured the senators, abstinence was simply not a practical option for young people.[20]

The Opposition Steps Forth

Predictably, the liberal Clintonistas on the Senate Committee confirmed the loudmouthed Dr. Joycelyn Elders for her high-level appointment as U.S. Surgeon General. But many concerned Americans have dedicated themselves to actively opposing the extremist policies she is espousing for the nation.

Pat Trueman, director of governmental affairs for the American Family Association, expressing dismay over Dr. Elders' anti-morality stance, has remarked, "She should be *discouraging* prostitution and drug abuse . . . Joycelyn Elders has an agenda that is non-medical and unbecoming for the position of Surgeon General."[21]

The respected *Christian Crusade* newspaper editorialized, "Dr. Elders' lack of a moral rudder and servitude to political correctness is troubling. She stands for everything that most Christians reject."[22]

"The culture wars heat up," wrote national columnist William Murchison. "As usual, Bill Clinton (in choosing Dr. Elders for her post) aligns himself with the bureaucrats and 60's retreads, laboring to reshape "worn-out" values like chastity and modesty."[23]

Conservative columnist Susan Fields also wrote a thoughtful column in which she reported:

> As chief presidential spokesman on the nation's health, the Surgeon General wields a different sort of power: The power of ideas. In choosing Dr. Elders, whose radical ideas on social policy set her far outside the mainstream, Mr. Clinton has once again managed to take a step away from the beliefs and concerns of ordinary Americans.[24]

Also commenting on Elders' nomination, Kay Cole James, the articulate vice president of the Family Research Council, remarked, "I'm a mother of three teenagers and this nominee scares me." James, a black woman whose meritorious achievements as assistant secretary for public affairs at the U.S. Department of Health and Human Services during the Bush administration were widely recognized, states that she is particularly alarmed over Dr. Elders' fanatical support for school-based clinics, sex instruction, and condom giveaways for underage children.[25]

Pointing out Dr. Elders' radical, pro-abortion views,

Reverend Dee Davis of the Harvest Church International in Washington, D.C., has declared, "We oppose the nomination . . . she's proven she's insensitive to the unborn."[26]

Notably, Reverend Davis, like Elders an African-American, wore a button with the message, "Abortion is Black Genocide," on her lapel, significant because Dr. Elders has often sought to make abortion a racial issue.

Elders Wages War on Christians

Is Reverend Davis correct? Is Dr. Joycelyn Elders "insensitive to the unborn?" You better believe it. Consider, for example, the fact that she once sneeringly barked, "pro-lifers are really going to have to get over their love affair with the fetus."[27]

Elders has only contempt for Christians. With a deceiving smile and a judgmental and politically correct snarl, she once told an audience that pro-life Christian leaders are "very religious non-Christians" who have "slave master mentalities."[28]

"Preachers have been moralizing for years," Elders sneered, when asked by a member of Arkansas' joint budget committee to comment about the rising chorus of protests of her policies by Christian ministers and clergy.[29]

At a U.S. Capitol protest against Dr. Elders' nomination, a number of African-American men and women pleaded with Congress not to confirm her for the job. Said Robin McDonald, a Washington, D.C. black woman who's also a social worker active in working with teenagers, "My concern is that they not pick someone because she's African-American. They should pick someone who represents the value of Americans at large."[30]

Fascist Views Unmasked

Many health professionals are distressed that such an incompetent, Nazi-like headmaster is now America's health overseer. Dr. Mildred F. Jefferson, assistant clinical professor of surgery at Boston University's School of Medicine, was so upset over Dr. Elders' extremist and fascist views that she requested to testify before the senate panel. Comparing Elders' ideas to those of the late fascist and Aryan race promoter Margaret Sanger, the notoriously racist founder of Planned Parenthood, Dr. Jefferson, a black woman, warned that Dr. Elders "parrots the Margaret Sanger social planning movement."[31]

"This," she added, "is the worst appointment that could be made for this position."[32]

Liberals Love This Woman's Ideas

Naturally, Joycelyn Elders has supporters as well as critics. Her shrill condemnations of conservative Christians and her mocking of pro-life believers have made Elders a heroine in the eyes of the wild-eyed, liberal crowd.

One such fervent supporter is Betty Bumpers, wife of U.S. Senator Bumpers from Arkansas. Mrs. Bumpers is, among other things, a fan of One World Government, which she thinks is a "logical progression" from our current American sovereignty. She's director of Peace Links, a pacifist group which has often supported Marxist causes and has, in the past, promoted warm relations with the (then communist) U.S.S.R.[33]

Another liberal feminist who waxes hot for Dr. Elders is none other than Rosalynn Carter, the former first lady.[34] This is to be expected, however, of the wife of the man who presided over one of the most disastrous, liberal White House administrations in American history. Social activist Jimmy Carter was such a colossal failure as president that the voters promptly put him out to pasture after suffering through four monstrously painful years. Hopefully, the same fate awaits the Hillbillary administration.

Perhaps the most scary of statements that have been made in support of Dr. Elders come from a black supporter,

Dr. Henry Foster, Jr., Dean of the School of Medicine at a medical college in Tennessee. "As Surgeon General," Foster wrote in a Nashville newspaper column, "Dr. Elders will deliver her message persuasively. She will maximize this health care bully pulpit which the position of Surgeon General affords."[35]

Now that's ominous—to realize that this outspoken, absurdly outrageous sponsor of safe sex for pre-schoolers now has the advantage of ranting, raving, and raging from one of America's premier *"bully pulpits."*

Hillary Has Her Reasons

Why did Hillary and Bill Clinton choose such an obnoxious, power-hungry bureaucrat for such an important position? The immediate answer is simple: Joycelyn Elders perfectly mirrors Hillary's ultra-radical views favoring lesbianism, homosexuality, aggressive promotion and taxpayer funding of abortions; and lax policies on the sale, possession, and use of illegal drugs.

Elders is yet another of Hillary's Hellcats—a militant and vulgar Amazon warrior who has dedicated her life and work to overthrowing traditional American values.

Elders, not surprisingly, is also a gun control nut just like her benefactors, Hillary and Bill. Though it would seem that firearms legislation would not exactly be the most essential of *health* issues, in an effort to win kudos from the Clintons and from her other femiNazi liberal pals, Elders has made this topic one of her pet projects. (That is, when she's not out promoting her *favorite* pet project: condoms and sex education in schools).

"Every day 135,000 youngsters take guns to school, more than 100 are shot, and 30 are killed," she lamented to the Journal of the American Medical Association. "The National Center for Health Statistics reports that more than 4,000 teenagers were killed by firearms in 1990."[36]

As wacky as this woman is, watch for Dr. Elders to

propose a new national program very soon for our public schools—something on the order of a "swap your gun for a condom" campaign.

Cover-up: The Dark Side of Joycelyn Elders

There's also yet another, less politically correct, reason why the Clintons decided on Joycelyn Elders to be our czarina of health affairs. Perhaps we can better understand her rabid criticism of people whom she dismisses as slaves of "ignorance and the Bible-belt mentality" when we examine a dark side of Dr. Elders that is demonstrably sleazy.

Case in point: her rescue of one Dr. Fahmy Malak, formerly Arkansas' controversial state medical examiner. Malak's reputation suffered blow-after-blow in the 80s. In three major cases, his autopsies were found to be faulty and he was overruled by juries. Dr. Malak was also challenged by other pathologists 17 times; and on one occasion, a crime-lab photographer revealed that the doctor had ordered him to fake photographs to create evidence.[37]

Dr. Fahmy Malak's career was definitely on the downslide and his dismissal seemed a strong possibility when, presto!, Dr. Joycelyn Elders came galloping to his rescue. Not only did the Czarina help exonerate her colleague of charges of gross incompetence, she actually recommended the embattled medical bureaucrat for a raise! When he was forced out of office anyway, she hired him to head up her state health department's AIDS programs—a position created out of thin air even though it violated a governmental hiring freeze.[38]

Why would Elders be so incredibly eager to reward such a tainted fellow? Ah! Now comes the sickest part of the story. It just so happens that it was this very same medical doctor who, as the state medical examiner, had previously investigated and cleared of wrongdoing a certain anesthetist also charged with gross incompetence.

In 1981, this anesthetist had failed to follow a surgeon's order to move a breathing tube from a patient's nose to her throat. As a result, the patient died. Reportedly, this was by no means the first problem encountered with this woman's professional work habits.

Her medical superiors and co-workers fully expected that the anesthetist would lose her license and be terminated due to her demonstrated careless and dangerous behavior and her proven incompetence. How surprised they must have been to get the news that the charges against this person were abruptly dropped by state authorities after good old Dr. Fahmy Malak "declined" to even investigate the matter.

They must have concluded the obvious: that the reason for the cover-up was that the anesthetist's name was *Virginia Dwyer*. Ms. Dwyer, of course, just happens to be Bill Clinton's mother whose current name is Virginia Kelly. And of course, both Dr. Malak and Dr. Elders, as state officials, worked for Governor Bill Clinton and his co-chief executive, Hillary.[39]

Was Dr. Joycelyn Elders' overly generous treatment of the discredited Dr. Fahmy Malak a payoff for his help in clearing Clinton's mother, Ms. Dwyer, of charges that, if substantiated and prosecuted, could have seriously damaged Bill and Hillary's future election chances?

And More Scandals . . .

Dr. Elders has also been involved in a highly suspect banking scandal. As a member of the board of directors for the once powerful National Bank of Arkansas in North Little Rock, she was in a position where she could possibly have funneled questionable bank loans to political supporters of herself, Hillary and Bill.

In fact, in March 1982, after problem loans were identified by bank regulators, Dr. Elders and eight other former directors were sued by the bank for $1.5 million in an attempt to recoup from "losses and bad loans" resulting from the mismanagement of Elders and her cohorts.[40]

A Lightning Bolt From Heaven

Dr. Joycelyn Elders is not deterred by her critics. She dismisses all arguments about her radical positions as "nonsense," and she glories in bragging that she's willing to take the heat to get her programs implemented throughout America. Elders calls herself a *"lightning rod"* and proudly wears a *lightning bolt pin* to demonstrate her defiance of Christian values.[41]

How fascinating! Bible students might recall that the lightening bolt is a symbol for *Lucifer, or Satan*. Here is how Jesus depicted man's dark-hearted adversary:

> And He said unto them, I beheld Satan as lightning fall from heaven (Luke 10:18).

RUTH BADER GINSBURG

Position: Supreme Court Justice

Moniker: *The Scarlet Judge*

"**R**uth Bader Ginsburg: A Mainstream Justice," blared the *USA Today* headline.[1]

"Clinton Selects Ginsburg, a Moderate, for the Supreme Court," wrote Robert Rankin in a nationally syndicated story for the Knight-Ridder News Service."[2]

"Ruth Ginsburg Has a Record of Judicial Restraint," crowed *Newsweek* magazine.[3]

Who were these liberal news reporters trying to kid? Ruth Bader Ginsburg *mainstream?* . . . a *moderate?* Come on, guys, as Abraham Lincoln once said, "You can fool all of the people some of the time, and some of the people all of the time, but you can't fool *all* of the people *all* of the time!"

In reality, Ginsburg is possibly *the most* radical liberal who has ever been appointed to the U.S. Supreme Court in the history of our august nation. What other kind of judge would you expect a Hillary and Bill administration to pick, anyway?

Her Scarlet Record

Let's take a close look at her scarlet record and *you* decide if the biased news media is simply trying to pull one over on we, the people.

R.E. McMaster, in his insight-filled *The Reaper* newsletter writes:

> Clinton picked Judge Ruth Bader Ginsburg for his first Supreme Court vacancy. She is a one-time crusader for women's rights ... Ginsburg was a liberal during her years as a practicing attorney which included seven years as general counsel for the American Civil Liberties Union. She is Jewish, from Harvard, and spent time at the Aspen Institute.[4]

The *American Civil Liberties Union (ACLU)*, as we shall see, is one of America's premier Christian and U.S. Constitution bashing organizations. Left-wing to its core, this is a bad, bad bunch of people.

The *Aspen Institute*, meanwhile, is notorious for its black reputation as a New Age and pro-New World Order think tank.

McMaster also reveals that Ginsburg is married to Professor Martin Ginsburg of Georgetown University Law School. Ginsburg is Ross Perot's tax attorney.[5] Here we have two insights: first, there's the Georgetown connection (*a la* Carroll Quigley, professor at Georgetown University and mentor of

Bill Clinton, who *admitted* his involvement in a global conspiracy of the super rich to control humanity).

Second, we find the same old entanglements of the rich with the rich—in this case, Ginsburg with Perot. Perot was catapulted into riches by New York's former Governor, Nelson Rockefeller, who, in the 60s, awarded Perot's upstart Electronic Data Services Corporation (EDS) a whopping state contract worth almost a billion dollars. That little favor put EDS and Perot on the map. It was this same Rockefeller combine that made Clinton a star, first down in Arkansas, and later, nationally.

Financial and political birds of a feather *do* flock together, don't they?

Twilight Zone Reasoning

I also credit McMaster with this shocking news flash:

> The new Supreme Court Justice, Ruth Bader Ginsburg, wrote in 1977 that women must be drafted into the military service any time men are, that there was a need for affirmative action for women in the armed forces, that the age of consent for sexual acts should be lowered to 12 years, that the equality principle requires that prostitution be legalized or decriminalized, that the Boy Scouts and Girl Scouts must change their names to be sex integrated to conform to the equality principle and eliminate stereotype sex roles, that the equality principle requires college fraternities and sororities to be sex integrated into social societies, that the concept of bread winner-husband, homemaker-wife must be eliminated from the code if it is to reflect the equality principle.[6]

Now, let's digest these insane, Twilight Zone rulings and bizarre, space cadet philosophies one at a time. According to Ginsburg, whom the Clintons and the liberal media tout is a "moderate," something which she fondly likes to call the "equality principle" essentially means that:

1. Women must be drafted into military service in the same ratio as men—that's what liberal thinkers call "quotas."
2. Women in the armed forces should be given preferential promotions and advancement regardless of merit—that's what liberal crazies call "affirmative action."
3. Pedophiles and vulgar sex perverts should have the right to lure and sexually seduce children of, say, 12 or 13 years of age—that's what liberal fruitcakes call "children's rights."
4. College fraternities and sororities have to be sexually integrated so that young men and women can all live happily together in the same dorms—that's what liberal weirdos call "sexual equality."
5. Husbands can no longer be the prime wage earner for families and wives should not be the homemakers—that's what liberal oddballs call "nuke the family."

If John Marshall, America's first Chief Justice of the Supreme Court were alive today, he'd vomit over the liberal judicial philosophies held so dear by Ms. Ginsburg. And so would George Washington, the Christian man and president who appointed Mr. Marshall to the federal bench.

Beyond Belief

Ginsburg's rulings are simply beyond belief—at least 90 percent of the American public would be aghast if they discovered the truth about her, but this has been conveniently covered up by the *New York Times, The Washington Post, CBS, ABC, NBC, etc.* Perhaps the reason why is that the chief executives of each of these media empires are, like their counterpart Ruth Bader Ginsburg, card-carrying members of the Council on Foreign Relations. That's right, Justice Ginsburg is a member of the CFR, the globalist nut factory that plots to end American sovereignty and merge the United States into what will eventually become a world dictatorship.

Yes, political birds of a feather *do* flock together.

Our U.S. Senate, whose members long ago sold their greedy souls for filthy lucre, confirmed Ms. Ginsburg by an overwhelming vote of 100 to nothing. Yet, *Human Events* noted that in 1981 Ginsburg had, as a federal judge, defied the Senate in a sweeping decision, in the case of Wright vs. Reagan.[7]

In that case, Ginsburg ordered the Internal Revenue Service (IRS) to impose on the nation's private schools harsh, new quota-based, "affirmative action" regulations. This in spite of the fact that the Congress had earlier adopted legislation to *ban* the use of federal funds to implement quota systems.

Ginsburg didn't let little things like the law or judicial precedent stop her from going on a liberal rampage, however. In violation of the statutes, she directed the IRS enforcers to deny tax exempt status to Christian and other private schools that did not comply with her tyrannical order.

In fact, Ginsburg was so wildly out of control in her punitive decision that, eventually, even a liberal U.S. Supreme Court majority overturned her flawed liberal ruling.

Child Sex With Adults OK?

Perhaps the most compelling reason why Ruth Bader (notice that, like her mentor, Hillary, Ruth insists on using her maiden name, Bader) Ginsburg may be unfit to serve on the U.S. Supreme Court or, for that matter, even as municipal judge for the tiny village of Podunk, Idaho, is her warped view of what is and what isn't consensual sex by adults with minors. In his excellent monthly newsletter, Dr. Charles Provan of the highly respected American Freedom Movement described his group's concern about Ginsburg's philosophy:

> Particularly disturbing, given Ginsburg's current nomination to the highest court in the land, is the reason she gave for opposing laws "controlling sexual behavior between adults and minors"—that statutory rape statutes are of "questionable constitutionality."

As stated on page 30 of the (court's formal) minutes . . ."In the second paragraph of the policy statement, Ruth Bader Ginsburg made a notion to eliminate the sentence reading: 'The state has a legitimate interest in controlling sexual behavior between adults and minors.' She argued that this implied approval of statutory rape statutes, which are of questionable constitutionality."[8]

This is sick, sick, but it seems to affirm the prevailing, pro-pervert agenda of the lesbian/homosexual forces embraced so warmly by people like Ruth Ginsburg and Hillary Clinton. Want proof? The following quotations are taken *verbatim* from the gay press and from documents authored by gay activists. These are also the pro-pedophilia demands of some of the gay participants of the April 25, 1993, gay "March on Washington," an event which was warmly applauded by President Bill Clinton:

NAMBLA'S (the North American Man/Boy Love Association's) position on sex is not unreasonable, just unpopular . . . The love between men and boys is at the foundation of homosexuality. (Editorial: "No Place for Homophobia," in the *San Francisco Sentinel*, one of that city's three, main gay newspapers).[9]

We demand . . . The implementation of laws that recognize sexual relations among youth, between consenting peers.[10]

It appears that the issue of extending "children's rights," as promoted by Ginsburg and the other hellcats in Hillary's feminist battalion of gay and liberal activists, means that, over the next few years, statutory rape laws in all 50 states will come under attack. Already, in Florida this year, a liberal judge has made a ruling which could become a precedent for the entire nation. As reported in *The Evangelical Methodist*:

Adult men have a fundamental right to have sex with underage girls, a Florida lower court judge has ruled. "If this constitutional right to privacy extends to the decision of a minor to have an abortion, it must extend to the decision to engage in sexual intercourse," said Judge Jerry Lockett, referring to a 1990 state high court decision holding that a minor girl has the right to abortion without her parent's knowledge.

Two 15-year old girls in the case told the court they *wanted* to have sexual relations with their (older adult) friends . . . and that they did not want them prosecuted for rape.[11]

Examine carefully the statement above: The judge ruled that if a minor can legally obtain an abortion without her parent's consent or knowledge, the young girl should *also* be able to legally and permissibly have sex with whomever she desires. What's more, it was the child's *rights* the judge claimed he was protecting.

This is nothing less than legalized child molestation foisted upon our kids by raving maniacs of the left wing.

Now we see the witches brew that is concocted for America's youth by Hillary's Hellcats: abortion rights for young girls means that we must sanction the "right" for young girls to have sex with adult men! This is the *children's rights* horror being unleashed by Hillary and her friends Marian Edelman, Donna Shalala, and Ruth Ginsburg.

Abortion on Demand—By Kids!

Ginsburg's views on abortion are extremely radical. Not only does she strongly favor abortion, Ginsburg claims that neither the federal government nor the states can restrict abortions on demand. Teenagers, too, should be able to *choose* to abort and kill their babies—without being counseled and without a parent knowing about it.

Moreover, Ginsburg has frequently been quoted as stating that, if she had gotten *her* way back when *Roe v. Wade* was first promulgated, there would not be a continuing political dispute over this controversial issue. She would, she implied, have written the decision so tightly that the pro-life community would have been permanently squelched. Now that's a real, unbiased *moderate* for you, isn't it?

Ginsburg's Senate Hearings Closed to the Public

Evidently, Senator Joseph Biden, the liberal democrat who chairs the Senate Judiciary Committee, knew that Ginsburg's radical views in favoring the legalization of adult-child sex, unlimited abortion on demand, and the demolition of such American, "Mom and apple pie" groups as the Girl Scouts and Boy Scouts, would inflame an informed citizenry and cause her nomination to be abruptly derailed.

No problem, Biden and his White House counterparts decided, *we'll just close the hearings to the public* so the people will never discover the awful future that lies in store for them once Ginsburg is given a *lifetime appointment* on the Supreme Court.

And that is exactly what happened. Here's an account of this treachery, as reported in *USA Today*:

> Supreme Court nominee Ruth Bader Ginsburg will appear in a closed session July 23 before the Senate Judiciary Committee to avoid public spectacles like the 1991 Clarence Thomas hearings, committee chairman Joseph Biden, D-Del., said Thursday. Public hearings on the Ginsburg nomination begin July 20.

> Biden said he wanted to make such sessions routine for future hearings to protect the Senate and nominees from potentially damaging information, unproven allegations and partisan attacks. He described the "recent contentiousness of the confirmation process" as "troubling," adding that "the purpose of the session will be to ask nominees face to face, on the record, under oath, about any investigative matter that has been raised . . ."

Jane Kirtley, executive director of the Reporters Committee for Freedom of the Press, said the change would lead to more trouble. "I don't see how they seriously can believe, after the American public had the experience of seeing the Clarence Thomas hearings live on television, that they will stand for closed proceedings."[12]

Well, unfortunately, Jane Kirtley, quoted above, was wrong. The liberal media was able to censor and block out the travesty of the senate panel holding closed hearings which deny the citizens of this once free nation the opportunity to judge for themselves the fitness for the nation's highest court of a candidate. Of course, when Clarence Thomas, *a conservative*, was nominated for the court, the liberals on the Senate Committee and their friends in the media put the judge through hell, grilling him unmercifully on national television and accusing him of the most hideous, unsubstantiated charges.

Ruth Ginsburg, the ACLU, and Communism

One of the most frightening demonstrations of Ms. Ginsburg's moral and ideological unfitness for high office is the fact that for seven long years she was general counsel to what has to be one of the most unAmerican and unChristian organizations on the face of the earth: the American Civil Liberties Union (ACLU). Some people in the know refer to the ACLU as *Atheists, Communists, and Lawyers United*— and rightly so, considering the pitiful, corrupt history of this terrible group of degenerates.

In his *Prophecy in the News* publication, J.R. Church gave this report on the ACLU-Ruth Ginsburg connection:

"The Truth About the ACLU

Since Ruth Bader Ginsburg was a longtime member of the ACLU, we thought you would like to know the background of this seditious organization.

The American Civil Liberties Union is having a tremendous impact on the American legal system. Their influence is felt in every corner of our culture.

Who are these people? Where did they come from and what do they stand for? The answers to these questions are shockingly revealing.

The History of the ACLU

The ACLU was founded as the *Bureau for Conscientious Objectors* of the *American Union Against Militarism* in 1917 by Roger Baldwin. The name was changed to the *Civil Liberties Bureau* later that year. It separated from the AUAM in October of 1918 and became the *National Civil Liberties Bureau*.

On August 31, 1918, the Bureau was raided by the police. They were searching for evidence of subversive materials. On November 11, 1918, Roger Baldwin began serving a one year term in federal prison for sedition.

When he was released, Baldwin renamed the Bureau the *American Civil Liberties Union*.

Today, the ACLU has 250,000 members, 70 staff lawyers, and 5,000 volunteer attorneys. It has an annual budget of $14 million and handles an average of 6,000 cases at any one time.

Who is Behind the ACLU?

Several of the ACLU's original executive board members were later prominent leaders in the Communist Party USA. These include William Foster, Elizabeth Gurley Flynn, and Louis Budenez. Roger Baldwin himself said, "I am for Socialism, disarmament, and ultimately for abolishing the state itself as an instrument of violence and compulsion. I seek social ownership of property . . . Communism is the goal." Baldwin also wrote in defense of Joseph Stalin.

In more recent years, the National Board has read like a Who's Who of the American Left. It has included (although not all of these people are currently serving): George McGovern, Norman Lear, Ed Asner, Julian Bond, Carl Sagan, Susan Estrich, Patricia Schroeder, Kurt Vonnegut, Norman Cousins, Ramsey Clark, Harriet Pilpel, Birch Bayh, Henry Steele Commager, Arthur Schlessinger, Lowell Weicker, Burt Lancaster, Ira Glasser, Alan Reitman, Norman Dorsen, Morton Halperin, and Sis Farenthold.

Does the ACLU Support Liberty?

That depends on who you are, and whether or not you agree with their political agenda.

While the ACLU has been involved with a few commendable causes, the overall picture is one of an organization bent on reforming American society according to the wisdom of liberalism.

The ACLU has defended the "free speech rights" of Nazis, child pornographers, Satanists, and the Ku-Klux-Klan. Yet they have refused to help anti-abortion protesters who were the victims of unlawful arrest and police brutality.

The ACLU's religious intolerance is a matter of public record. In recent years they have sought to:

- Stop the singing of Christmas carols like "Silent Night" and "Away in a Manger" in public facilities.
- Deny tax-exempt status to churches while maintaining it for themselves and for various occultic groups.
- Disallow prayer, not just in public school classrooms, but also in locker rooms, sports arenas, graduation exercises, and legislative assemblies.
- Terminate all military and prison chaplaincies; Deny children in Christian schools access to publicly funded services.
- Eliminate nativity scenes, crosses, and other Christian symbols from public property.
- Repeal all "blue law" statutes.
- Prohibit voluntary Bible reading in public schools--even during free time or after classes.
- Remove *In God We Trust* from our coins.
- Deny accreditation to science departments at Bible believing Christian universities.
- Prevent the posting of the Ten Commandments in classrooms.
- Terminate voucher programs and tuition tax credits.
- Prohibit census questions about an individual's religious affiliation.
- Purge the words *under God* from the Pledge of Allegiance.

The ACLU Supports:

- Legalization of child pornography.
- Tax exemption for Satanists.
- Legalization of prostitution.
- Abortion on demand.

- Mandatory sex education.
- Forced busing of children.
- Ideological testing for court nominees.
- Automatic entitled probation.
- Public demonstrations for Nazis and communists.
- Legalization of polygamy.

The ACLU Opposes:

- Voluntary school prayer.
- Sobriety checkpoints.
- Religious displays in public.
- Tax exemptions for churches.
- Medical safety regulations and reporting.
- Parental consent laws.
- Educational vouchers and home schooling.
- Governmental ethics committees.
- Prison terms for criminal offenses.
- Public demonstrations for direct-action pro-lifers.
- Teaching "monogamous, heterosexual intercourse within marriage" in the public schools."[13]

And More Insanity by the ACLU

Considering the above, it's no wonder that patriotic Americans and concerned Christians are worried about the damage that Ruth Ginsburg will bring to this country as a Supreme Court Justice.

And here's more disturbing evidence that Ginsburg's seven year long affair as top lawyer for the smutty ACLU disqualifies her for *any* judgeship, let alone the highest court in the land:

* *ACLU Convinces Postmaster to End Nazareth's Christmas Mark*: The ACLU grinches who stole Christmas! The small community of Nazareth, Texas simply wanted to spread Christmas joy and so the local post office offered a special commemorative postmark, drawn by local artist Rosemary Wilhelm, depicting a nativity scene and doves of

peace. But the ACLU's director called for "an immediate end" to it. The U.S. Postmaster General caved in and within 30 minutes of the ACLU's demand, ordered Nazareth to discontinue the postmark.[14]

* *ACLU Fights Public Prayer*: In 1993, the Tennessee General approved a bill allowing public prayer at some school functions. The American Civil Liberties Union promptly threatened to challenge the new bill.

* *Sexual Abstinence Teachings Unconstitutional, ACLU Says.* In 1993, when the Georgia State Board of Education unanimously voted to emphasize abstinence in sex education, a furious ACLU went through the roof. "It is our position," said the ACLU, "that teaching monogamous heterosexual intercourse within marriage as a traditional American value is an unconstitutional establishment of a religious doctrine in public schools."[15] (And America doesn't understand why out-of-wedlock, teenage pregnancies are at an all-time high!?)

In Summary . . .

So, here's the bottom line: Ruth Bader Ginsburg is yet another of Hillary's revolutionary women whose extremist views flaunt America's traditional values. Immoral people, ranging from child molesters to the most vile of late term abortion doctors, are rejoicing that one of their "sisters" now has the power to implement their sick and foul sexual/ socialist agenda. But true, sensitive Americans everywhere who love their children and want their families to prosper and succeed, must now be on guard. The walls are bulging, and only through diligent and courageous, even heroic efforts, will we be able to stem the quickening tidal wave of darkness and debauchery to be unleashed by the Clinton Supreme Court.

TIPPER GORE

Position: Wife of the Vice President

Moniker: *Ms. Rock 'N Roll*

During the race for president, the mass media portrayed Hillary and Tipper as the most delightful and chummy of pals. On stage at the Democrat Party's national convention, as network TV cameras whirred, they embraced and hugged, and, with arms locked, Tipper and Hillary endearingly danced a round or two. Then, the two women struck out by bus across America on the campaign trail with their spouses, Bill and Al.

That was then. Now is now, and rarely are the first and second "ladies" seen in public together. Co-Chief Executive Hillary Rodham Clinton is far too high and mighty to associate with a common housewife like Tipper.

To add insult to slight, Hillary has quite obviously superseded Tipper's husband, the Vice President, in the minds of the massive federal bureaucracy. Though traditionally in federal offices the framed pictures of the President and Vice President often hang side-by-side, visitors to federal office buildings have reported seeing Hillary's picture instead of Al Gore's on walls beside that of her hubby, Bill Clinton's.

Meanwhile, unlike Dan Quayle who, as Vice President, was delegated considerable authority by President George Bush, poor Al Gore has been relegated to the dung pile of political inactivity. The Clinton White House insists that poor Al Gore, affectionately known as the "Ozone Man," has not been assigned important posts because he's far too valuable to the president as a "close advisor." But Washington insiders know different.

Meanwhile, Big Sister Hillary Clinton has been given a suite of offices in the powerful West Wing of the White

House from which she commands immense influence to get things done.

Tipper Appeals to the Bible Belt

Tipper, like so many other wives of ambitious politicos, has paid a heavy price for her 15 minutes of fame. She's also demonstrated that, like her superior, Hillary, she's more than willing to waffle and to compromise her integrity when political expediency dictates.

In the 1980s, as the wife of a U.S. Senator from Tennessee—a southern, family values-oriented state located smack in the epicenter of the Bible Belt, Tipper put on a convincing display in her acting roles of "Christian Fundamentalist" and "Defender of the Traditional Family." For example, sensing that the citizens of Tennessee, like so many other Americans, were fed up with satanic vulgarity and hard core, sexually explicit lyrics on rock music albums, she founded an ostensibly family-oriented, national campaign to force executives of the top record labels to print warning notices on their albums to help parents determine which music contains filthy lyrics.

Perverted rock star Frank Zappa and leaders of many other rock bands, as well as a multitude of liberal political groups, blasted Tipper Gore, accusing her of being a narrow-minded censor and of attempting to deny people in the music industry their constitutional right to free speech. The name "Tipper" became a curse word to rock stars who harshly branded Gore "America's #1 threat to freedom and liberty."

However, thousands of letters in support of her strong position opposing filthy music poured into Tipper's mail box and the Senator's office. Therefore, to further seize political advantage, Tipper arranged for a ghost writer to pen a book for her on the subject. Printed and distributed by a well-known Christian publisher, Abingdon Press, the book, *Raising PG Kids In An X-Rated Society*, became an immediate bestseller throughout the Christian community.

A Fundamentalist Superstar

Suddenly, Tipper Gore was a *fundamentalist Christian superstar!* She was in great demand by Christian radio and talk show hosts and television evangelists who sought to interview her. Pastors of conservative doctrine churches besieged Tipper with requests for appearances and speaking engagements.

Meanwhile, just as the Gores figured, the polls back home showed that Tipper had struck a responsive chord among Tennessee's electorate, angry over satanic and pornographic rock music and wary as they were about America's rapidly declining moral values. Her opposition to the sick music and the degenerate, heavy metal rock stars who have for so long subverted and undermined the morals of our youth and sullenly seduced them into rebellion and anarchy had won points for Tipper among the hardworking, God-fearing majority of Tennessee's fine citizens.

Emboldened by their rising popularity back home, resulting from their support of this conservative Christian cause, the Gores also decided to take on another moral crusade: *they joined the fight against abortion.* Senator Gore began to assure the heads of pro-life organizations and concerned church leaders that he, too, was deeply committed to the cause of pro-life and would forever remain a firm opponent of the killing of unborn babies.

In a letter to a constituent in 1987, Senator Gore affirmed his support in Congress for Representative Henry Hyde's pending bill to ban the use of federal funds for abortions. Gore wrote:

> During my 11 years in Congress, I have consistently opposed federal funding of abortions. In my opinion, it is wrong to spend federal funds for what is, arguably the taking of a human life.

> Let me assure you that I share your belief that innocent human life must be protected, and I am committed to furthering this goal.[1]

Senator Gore, like his wife, Tipper, found himself in great demand to speak before Christian audiences. Some conservative pastors even trekked to Washington, D.C. to visit the Senator in hopes they could get their pictures taken with him.

The Big Reversal

In the summer of 1992, the political fortunes of Tipper and Al shifted dramatically and suddenly on the day it was announced that Al Gore would be Bill Clinton's running mate. New social and political conditions prevailed, and to appease the crazy, spaced-out liberals who dominate the Democrat Party, Tipper and Al were prepared to make a 180° reversal in their positions on such issues as filth and decadence in rock music and on the immorality of abortion.

Al Gore immediately began to depict himself as a lifetime supporter of the radical, pro-choice, abortion-on-demand position. He enthusiastically embraced the entire pro-abortion leadership and pledged his undying devotion to their cause. Unwanted babies had to go, said Al, the more the merrier. Women's privacy was at stake.

Tipper Gore, too, experienced a born again experience as a new, radical liberal. Asked repeatedly at campaign stops about her previous position on rock music lyrics, Tipper flip-flopped. She totally denied that she had ever favored restrictions! What's more, the wife of the prospective vice president of the United States publicly scoffed at the notion that her book, *Raising PG Kids In An X-Rated World*, was a "Christian" book.

Why, this never was a moral or religious issue at all, Tipper assured the press. *It was a feminist issue!* You see, Ms. Gore gingerly explained, she had become upset because there were so many *anti-woman lyrics* in rock music. That's all.

Tipper the Heavy Metal Fanatic

To prove once and for all to the doubting Thomases of the closed-minded, liberal community that she had really been one of them all along, Tipper and Al next began to dutifully take their teenage son, hand-in-hand, to heavy metal rock concerts. On one occasion, the Gore family showed up at a Grateful Dead rock concert. A smiling and chatty Tipper Gore touchingly told amused reporters that the Grateful Dead was her and Al's *favorite rock group.*

As Tipper and Al well know, the Grateful Dead is unquestionably one of America's sickest and most despicable satanic rock groups. In fact, one of their best known tunes is entitled "Friend of the Devil." For over a quarter of a century, the "Dead," as they're called by their adoring fans, have been preaching and pitching their depressing messages of dope, death, and the devil to thousand of groupies. Now, Tipper proudly identifies herself as one of those groupies.[2]

What is there about the Grateful Dead and their music that Tipper and Al so admire? Perhaps it's their attitude. Jerry Garcia, the dopehead band leader of the "Dead" admits that he has an "ornery" streak.[3]

"There's a part of me that has a *bad attitude*," he told a *Rolling Stone* interviewer. "It's like, F . . . . (expletive deleted) You!"[4]

Garcia also takes pride in the group's promotion of anarchy. "We're gearing up for the millennium," he explains, a time of "spiritual transformation." It's the New Age, he comments, and in the year 2012, we'll become immortal. We'll be "pure thought forms," not bodies. This theology, he remarks, "is much, much more visionary and sumptuous than, say, *Christ* is coming back."[5]

Somehow, the religious philosophy of the Grateful Dead's Jerry Garcia seems to blend in and mesh quite nicely with the New Age, paganistic theology of Albert Gore, as expressed in the Ozone Man's bestselling, but academically absurd, environmental epic, *Earth in the Balance.*

Funeral Pyres of the Grateful Dead

Law enforcement authorities have reported that everywhere the Grateful Dead perform, death and misery follow in their wake. Kids and adults by the tens of thousands have by now poked their veins with heroin, snorted cocaine, and popped LSD because it's the "in-thing" to do for Grateful Dead concert-goers and fans. Many have died of drug overdoses. No one has even bothered to keep statistics of all those "Dead" aficionados who, afflicted with satanic depression, have committed suicide.

The powerful hallucinogenic drug LSD has long played an important, but tragic, role in the lives and deaths of Grateful Dead fans. In *U.S.A. Today*, it was reported that:

> LSD now gets longer federal prison sentences than any other drug—10 years without parole for as little as $5 worth of LSD on sugar cubes . . . *About 500 LSD offenders, mostly young fans of the Grateful Dead rock band, are in federal prisons.*[6]

Five hundred young people are rotting in prison today because of the monstrously dark influence of the Grateful Dead. No one knows how many countless others over the years have been in and out of prisons. These men and women have had their lives wrecked and their souls scarred by America's premier satanic rock band. But Tipper and Al, at the height of the '92 presidential campaign, proudly took their young son to a concert of this depraved group and acclaimed it as their favorite!

Incredibly, Al even bought and, by his own admission, has worn on a number of occasions a psychedelic Grateful Dead tie which he bought during a concert from a souvenir vendor. He's even been pictured in rock magazines wearing the tie.

In Clinton's Name We Rock

None of this should surprise us. The hypocrisy of Hillary's Hellcats and the men around them is, by now, legend. Anyway, why wouldn't Tipper and Al groove to MTV videos and to heavy metal, devil rock music? Consider their mentors, Hillary and Bill. In *US* magazine, satanic rock band star Jon Bon Jovi raved about what a great president America now has:

> Bill Clinton's the first president who's not old enough to be my father, who understands rock 'n roll, who smoked dope . . . and avoided the draft. He did the things that I can relate to. He called me up last week. I spoke to him. That's pretty hip.[7]

HAZEL O'LEARY

Position: Secretary of Energy

Moniker: *Not Irish*

Patriotic financial advisor Franklin Sanders writes of Hazel O'Leary, "Some of us thought this appointment was a reward to Irish Democrats until we found out Mrs. O'Leary was black." He continues:

> She's another Carter retread, having served both President Ford and President Carter as a regulatoress in the U.S. Department of Energy. She has been working for a Minnesota utility, Northern Power, and is a big friend of natural gas.

Her husband (now deceased) was deputy secretary of energy under Carter.

Surprise, she's also a lawyer.[1]

It appears that, unlike most Clinton appointees who are darlings of the liberal crowd, O'Leary has significant opposition from the typical gaggle of radicals who congregate around Hillary and Bill. They're afraid she may not be liberal enough. The ultra-liberal Public Concern Foundation, in its *The Washington Spectator* newsletter, scathingly noted that O'Leary is "a millionaire."[2] That's almost a capital crime in some liberal circles, although the liberal groupies conveniently ignore the fact that virtually all of Hillary and Bill's appointees are super-rich millionaires. Most are lawyers, too; but of course, that is just fine with the chic liberals— they just love *liberal lawyers* who support socialist and Democrat causes.

The Washington Spectator also snidely criticized O'Leary because her former employer, Northern States Power, generates its electricity from coal and nuclear fuel. The environmental whackos are violently opposed to the coal and nuclear industries.

Public Citizen, yet another liberal watchdog group, quotes Ken Bassong, a former co-worker of O'Leary, as complaining that Clinton's female Secretary of Energy is "too deferential to the more conservative views of corporate and government officials."[3]

Most probably, Hazel O'Leary will survive the sniper attacks of her liberal critics. Her tenure is made more secure by the fact that the Rockefeller and Bilderberger interests who financially back the Clintons want to make sure one of their own is filling a post like Secretary of Energy that is so dear to their pocketbooks.

In addition—and equally important—is the fact that Mrs. O'Leary is black. Her appointment buttressed President Clinton's claim that he would appoint more minorities to top government offices. Her firing would likely be viewed as a betrayal of that promise and cause problems with black civil rights leaders who are fervent supporters of Hillary and Bill's administration.

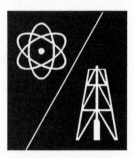

T A R A
O ' T O O L E

Position: Assistant Secretary of Energy

Moniker: Karla Marx

At the time this book went to press, the confirmation of Dr. Tara O'Toole had been held up by the U.S. Senate's Energy and Natural Resources Committee because of her affiliation with an aggressively liberal, feminist group that formerly characterized itself as "Marxist." Two members of the Senate panel expressed dismay over O'Toole's nomination by the Billary team.[1]

Senator Malcolm Wallop of Wyoming, the ranking Republican on the energy committee, accused President Clinton of nominating someone from "America's radical left fringe."[2] But isn't that like complaining that Santa Claus wears a red suit? *All* Santas have red suits! However, since a *majority* of Hillary and Bill's friends and appointees *do* have current or past ties to Marxist organizations and *they* have been confirmed, probably O'Toole will get the Senate's nod as well.

O'Toole is certainly no greater a Marxist believer than Hillary Rodham. Hillary, too, has a history of rather conspicuous associations with Communists, Socialists, and Marxists (the three types are generally in the same philosophical camp).

Her conservative critics point out that Dr. O'Toole, a physician who is now a "consultant" to the energy department, is a member of an unusual group of women crazies known as the *Northeast Feminist Scholars*. Originally, this far out group called itself by a more fitting name: *Marxist-Feminist Group I*.[3]

"We believe she is superbly qualified," William White, the deputy secretary of energy said of O'Toole. White says that the Clinton nominee is the target of unfair political aspersions.[4]

Oh sure. And Mickey Mouse isn't a friendly rodent, either.

JANET RENO

Position: Attorney General

Moniker: *Duchess of Doom*

Janet Reno is living proof that the inmates are now fully in charge of the insane asylum. What's more, the locos have convinced the outside world that it is their victims and not themselves who are crazy!

Consider these rather astute and extremely revealing comments by Dick Hafer who has researched and documented the lives and habits of Clinton appointees:

> Janet Reno is a woman of "unusual tastes." Unmarried, childless, and at 6'2," an imposing person, Ms. Reno relaxes in various ways.

One peculiar way is to lie on her trampoline in her backyard and recite (the famed poet Samuel) Coleridge . . . until she fell asleep, surrounded by 35 pet peacocks, who are ALL NAMED HORACE!

She also relaxes by chain sawing trees. (Does Al Gore know about this?) This is our nation's top law enforcement official?[1]

Hafer also refers to a colorful but mind-boggling feature story in *The Washington Post* which explains that, in Janet Reno's home, "There are dusty floors and a rusty refrigerator that closes with a latch hook." And a necklace of fossilized alligator droppings.[2]

Reno, *The Washington Post* article explains, "grew up with no air conditioning, no fans, no washer or dryer, and no television," though her parents were affluent and well-off financially. In her household, Reno and her parents "didn't practice religion, but they studied the Bible, Greek mythology, the stars."[3]

Her Failed Record as a Prosecuting Attorney

The fact that Janet Reno has some personal quirks and eccentricities does not necessarily make her unfit for high public office. If these were her only failings, we would have no real reasons to oppose her elevation to America's top law enforcement position. But the fact is, Ms. Reno's record as the state attorney and chief prosecutor for Miami and Dade County, Florida, is so incredibly deficient that it beggars the imagination.

Even the *Miami Herald*, a newspaper whose liberal editors adore Janet Reno and the Clintons, was forced to admit that her performance as a prosecutor was atrocious. "She has a losing record in the highest profile cases," the newspaper reported, adding: "Her office has been accused of lacking investigative zeal, often letting cases languish for years."[4]

How mind-jarring! This is the stone-faced, hatchet woman who wasted no time at all in *hurriedly* smashing down the walls of the Branch Davidian compound and putting a *rushed* and fiery end to the stand-off in Waco.

A reliable correspondent of mine from Miami told me that while Janet Reno was in charge of prosecuting criminals in that city and county, crime rose to disastrous proportions. "Miami," he said "became the drug-running, Mafia capital of the world during her years as state attorney."

Further proof of Reno's incompetence comes from Thurman Brown, a former federal investigator stationed in South Florida: "Miami's Brickell Avenue is now lined with glittering new banks full of drug money," says Brown.[5]

And what of the drug dealers who deposited all that money? "I don't think Reno has gone after a single one,"[6] he laments. "Her larger-than-life image as an honest prosecutor serves as a front—a cover-up to be blunt—for one of the most crime-ridden jurisdictions in the United States."[7]

According to Jeff Leen, the *Miami Herald's* respected investigative reporter, while Reno sat back idle and did little to stop crime, Florida's political and judiciary systems were rife with unbelievable corruption. In one year alone half of the judges in the Miami court system were under federal criminal investigation. Six judges were arraigned on bribery and extortion and, in one case, on murder charges.[8]

Now get this: none of these cases were brought by Reno, even though she had 230 lawyers under her direct supervision and reigned at the state's attorney post for 15 years. They were all *federal* cases, prosecuted by a crime fighting U.S. attorney appointed by the Bush administration.[9]

Reno A "Front-line Crime Fighter?"

Amazing as it may seem, when President Bill Clinton nominated Janet Reno as the nation's first female attorney general, he boasted that, "She is a front-line crime fighter and a caring public servant."[10] (Say what?!)

Now comes the truly astonishing part: On March 23, 1993, Janet Reno, as her first act as attorney general, promptly fired all 93 U.S. attorneys working for the Justice Department. Political insiders said it was probably to get rid of just one of them, Jay Stephens. He was Reno's only target, but to make it look good, she had to can all of them.[11]

Why Jay Stephens? Because at the time, he was on the verge of indicting Congressman Dan Rostenkowski, influential chairman of the House Committee that has life and death control over Bill Clinton's tax bills. Rostenkowski allegedly is involved in the embezzlement of monies of the House of Representatives post office.[12]

Slick Willie Clinton tried to justify Reno's actions, claiming that, "All of those people are routinely replaced with each incoming administration."[13]

Not so, responded Democratic Senator Daniel Moynihan: "It has been the norm since 1977 for U.S. attorneys to complete the remainder of their terms."[14]

Reno and Votescam

It wasn't the first time that Janet Reno has intervened in the political process to help a corrupt colleague in need. In their book, *Votescam: The Stealing of America*, two brothers who are investigative journalists from the Miami area, Jim Collier and Ken Collier, recount how, for nearly two decades, Prosecutor Janet Reno covered up rampant voter cheating and fraud in local elections. Voting machines were tampered with and rigged in hundreds of precincts so that only the "pre-approved candidates" would win election.[15]

After the *Home News*, a Dade County weekly, ran feature articles detailing this incredible and malignant scheme to rob the voters, the newspaper's publisher was shot as he walked up his driveway one evening. Janet Reno, as state attorney, never acted on the shooting and it is still listed officially as an "unsolved" crime.[16]

Unafraid for their own safety, the courageous Collier

brothers next distributed a shocking video, recorded clandestinely, which actually caught crooked poll volunteers of the League of Women Voters at a table, secretly punching holes in the punch cards intended only for voters. The video also captured Reno's cronies, including high political figures and even the Mayor, in the vote count room, which was legally supposed to be off-limits.[17]

Under pressure, the Governor of the state of Florida appointed well-known attorney Ellis Rubin as an omnsbudsman to investigate the allegations of vote fraud. Rubin's investigative report concluded that massive voting irregularities had occurred. The fraud was so bad, said Rubin, that it "shocked and sickened" him.[18]

However, even after Rubin's thorough report detailing voter fraud and abuse was issued, Janet Reno declined to look into the matter. For Reno, covering up and protecting her crooked political pals took precedence over insuring integrity and honesty at the voting booth.

So we find that Janet Reno not only has a kooky, alternative lifestyle, but she is proven to be incompetent and corrupt as a law enforcement officer. Sounds like a perfect candidate for Hillary to have chosen to be in charge of the huge and powerful Department of Justice, with an annual budget topping $11 billion and 84,000 employees spread throughout the United States and overseas. Perfect, that is, based on a comparison with Hillary's other cabinet choices.

Janet Reno A Queer Choice

Janet Reno has been called "a queer choice for attorney general." According to Florida Attorney Jack Thompson, the new attorney general is a hardened lesbian in the worst conceivable way. If Thompson is correct—and I have reason to believe he is—Janet Reno is a closet lesbian who is so wickedly, sexually corrupt that she has frequently used call girls for sex and, as Dade County, Florida attorney, she sexually harassed female county employees.[19]

If these charges were made by a less reputable person, they might be easily dismissed, but attorney Jack Thompson is known throughout the state of Florida as an honest Christian man and a brilliant trial lawyer. He is a member and elder of Key Biscayne Presbyterian Church, a congregation of the conservative Presbyterian Church in America (PCA).

When Jack Thompson discovered the extent of Reno's immorality and her demonstrated malfeasance in office, he felt it his duty to attempt to unseat her. In 1988, Thompson decided to run against her in the election of Dade County Attorney, a position that covers the metropolis of Miami. Although his bid was unsuccessful, he garnered more votes than any previous Reno opponent.

During the campaign, the courageous and bold Thompson confronted Reno at one of her public appearances by handing her a questionnaire and asking her to check the appropriate box declaring whether she was (1) homosexual; (2) bisexual; or (3) heterosexual.

Reno brushed aside the questionnaire, then grasped her opponent's shoulders, shook him, and said, "I like strong, virile, intelligent men." To which Thompson responded, "I like strong, virile, intelligent men, too, but I don't go to bed with them."[20]

Janet Reno's cutesy answer to the question of whether or not she is a lesbian obviously irritated lesbian activists. Later, in 1993, Reno again evaded this question, which was asked her by a reporter as she triumphantly arrived at Miami International Airport after being confirmed by the U.S. Senate for the attorney general slot. "I'm just an awkward old maid with a great affection for men," she said coyly.[21]

Margaret Cantrell, a spokeswoman for the radical gay Queer Nation group, which delights in "outing" closet lesbians, denouncing Reno for her cowardice, angrily complained, "She hasn't answered the question straight out. I like intelligent men, too. I *don't* sleep with them."[22]

Days later, representatives from Queer Nation, still unhappy with Reno's lame attempt to disassociate herself publicly with lesbianism, staged a public news conference at the steps of the Justice Department building. A spokesperson for the group declared: "Many homosexuals in Miami have contacted us and told us that Janet Reno's lesbianism is common knowledge among the gay community."[23]

The efforts by the lesbian activist group Queer Nation to force Janet Reno to come out of the closet and openly admit her lesbian sexual preference were rebuffed by Ms. Reno. Indeed, there was fear in the Clinton camp that Queer Nation's press conference might cause either an embarrassed White House to withdraw, or a fearful Senate Judiciary Committee to reject, Reno's nomination as attorney general.

To the rescue, however, came Patricia Ireland, the militant, gay lesbian head of the National Organization for Women (NOW). Ireland, who remains married to a man while also shacking up with a woman, told reporters: "Ms. Reno should not be judged on the basis of her sexual orientation."[24]

Thompson Hounded by Reno's Cronies

Attorney Jack Thompson says that he has been hounded and harassed by Reno's influential friends because of his attempts to expose her lurid behavior while in office. Reno's pals have illegally dispatched agents from the Florida Department of Law Enforcement to tail him. On one occasion, Reno's colleagues tried to have the Florida Bar Association disbar him. The scheme was to have Thompson declared "mentally incapacitated" because of his supposedly "obsessive" efforts opposing pornography.[25]

A psychologist crony of Reno's, who never even bothered to interview Thompson, diagnosed him as a "homophobe," a person whom gay activists define as one who "fears and hates homosexuals."

Thompson fought back with expert witnesses, including a respected psychiatrist who thoroughly vindicated him, gave him a clean bill of health, and stated that Thompson was simply a "Christian activist."

The Florida Bar, made up of attorneys, was forced not

only to dismiss the trumped-up charges against Jack Thompson, but to pay him $20,000 in a settlement, in acknowledgement of their lawless and wholly unethical, gulag attempt to discredit him.

All this caused Jack Thompson to quip, "I am now one of the few certified sane lawyers in Florida."

Reportedly, this was the first time in the history of the United States that a Bar Association was beaten in litigation and required to fork over money to an opponent it had unethically tried to destroy. Reno's blatantly sinister effort to intimidate Thompson had backfired.

A Pattern of Lesbian and Criminal Activity

Jack Thompson's investigation of Janet Reno has focused not only on her lesbian lifestyle, but also on other alleged criminal activity. Thompson says he has documented evidence that Reno has undergone extensive psychological counseling, that she was arrested for shoplifting lingerie at a Jordan March department store in 1981, and that she has a severe alcohol abuse problem.[26]

In written affidavits and orally, Thompson has also asserted that:

> . . . Washington reporter Mike Hedges called 20 of Reno's public supporters, and every single one of them has verified that Reno is widely reputed to be a homosexual.

> . . . Florida Senator Bob Graham, who was asked by President Clinton if he knew of any skeletons in Reno's closet, knows of the widely-held belief that one of Reno's lovers is ABC affiliate WPLG-TV's female news anchor, Ann Bishop.

> . . . A former assistant state attorney volunteered that while he was in Reno's office, senior assistant state attorneys helping with new employee's orientation would pull aside

each new hire and confide, in his words, "You'll be hearing, if you haven't already, stories that Janet Reno is a lesbian. She is, so don't act shocked, and just shrug your shoulders."

. . . A Miami police officer, Philip Buckman, told two witnesses that one night while on stakeout at *Sunday's*, a restaurant in Key Biscayne, he saw Ms. Reno enter with another woman, become drunk as the evening progressed, and begin "making out" passionately with her date.

. . . Reno uses *call girls* for sex. One such call girl, whose name is "Crystal," has reportedly told the publisher of a certain "escort" magazine that she has received money for sex from Reno at Reno's home.

. . . A homosexual talk show host has related that Reno was once apprehended by a Broward County police officer in a shopping mall parking lot in the back seat of a car with a disrobed young girl. After Reno identified herself as a district attorney, no criminal charges were filed.

. . . Reno has been pulled over five times in Dade County while driving "under the influence" of alcohol. This was reported by *five different police officers*. United States Senator Trent Lott's office has memoranda relating to the drunk driving investigation.

. . . Reno was once blackmailed by a homosexual, "shock radio" talk show host. The perverted homosexual radio personality was at the time *soliciting teen boys on the air for sex*. When her office was subsequently flooded with phone calls from irate citizens demanding she do something about this outrage, Janet Reno announced she would "open an investigation." The next day, however, she promptly closed the investigation after the homosexual talk show host referred repeatedly in his broadcast to Ms. Reno's own, peculiar sex habits.[27]

Senate Panel Not Interested

Now, if these allegations by Attorney Jack Thompson are true, it should have been a piece of cake for investigators of the Senate Judiciary Committee to determine the facts. Scores of actual eye witnesses to Janet Reno's unseemly behavior could have been made available to the Senate panel. Reno would have been quickly declared unfit to hold high office, especially the post of attorney general of the United States.

In fact, Jack Thompson *officially requested* the Senate Committee allow him to appear as a witness under oath. In a letter to Chairman Joseph Biden (D-Maryland), Thompson wrote, "I hereby put my good name, my entire legal career, my duties as a citizen and as a Christian compelled to tell the truth, on the line . . ."[28]

Thompson also provided the Senator with the names of at least 12 other reliable people who could testify as to the veracity of these things.

Instead of calling Jack Thompson as a witness, the corrupt chairman of the Senate Committee announced that he had the FBI investigate the charges by Thompson and others of misconduct by Janet Reno, and the FBI found them "unfounded and scurrilous."

This was the same liberal Senator whose committee, just a year previous, had unmercifully grilled Judge Clarence Thomas after the Judge was accused by Anita Hill of the most ridiculous of sexual harassment charges.

Thompson personally contacted each of the 12 people whose names he had furnished Senator Biden. He discovered that not one person of the 12 had been interviewed by the FBI. *Not one!* Obviously, Senator Biden simply had told a bald-faced lie to cover up his committee's disgraceful action in approving Ms. Reno for her high-ranking cabinet position.[29]

The national media, including top newspapers, news magazines *Time* and *Newsweek*, and the three major TV networks, have refused to investigate or report on Janet Reno's past record of lesbianism and her alleged criminal activities.

Yet, Attorney Jack Thompson refuses to back down. In fact, on a popular Miami talk show hosted by a fellow Christian, Mike Thompson (no relation), he issued this public challenge to Janet Reno: He challenged her to *sue him* for defamation and libel.

"You won't sue me, Janet," Thompson boldly announced, "because you know I'm telling the truth."[30]

Janet Reno and the Waco Massacre

It was her order to murder and burn alive the 86 members of the Branch Davidian religious group in Waco, Texas that earned for Ms. Reno my moniker of "Duchess of Doom." Possibly, she deserves a formal name change as well. Transposing the letters could produce the surname *Nero* instead of Reno. After all, it was the Emperor Nero who at first falsely accused the early Christians of vile acts, and then went on to burn the city of Rome to the ground and blame it on the innocent Christians.

Bill Clinton and Janet Reno insisted that they ordered the attack on the Waco compound because they were concerned that "child abuse" was going on. Well, they can rest easy now—those kids will never be abused again!

Here, then, is another recklessly dangerous attempt to commit a violent criminal act and then excuse its commission by saying, "I did it for the kids." Is this what Hillary and Bill Clinton, Donna Shalala, and their friend Janet Reno shamelessly call "children's rights?"

How the Government Abused the Kids

In fact, during the weeks of siege against the men, women, and children barricaded inside the Branch Davidian building and terrified for their lives, Janet Reno herself abused these kids over and over. She had armored personnel carriers and tanks run over and crush their go-carts and bicycles just outside their windows. She had her Gestapo agents play amplified, hideously occultic sounds of rabbits being slaughtered and Tibetan Buddhist monks chanting to their demon spirit guides, scaring the children and depriving them of sleep.[31]

Reno's SS brigade held the press back to a three mile distance so no one could find out the awful facts about her mental and physical torture of these helpless children. She then cut off their food, their milk, their water, their electricity, their plumbing. At night she bombarded their bedroom windows with blinding, high-intensity lights.

She left the dead body of one man, a Branch Davidian killed by her agents, hanging for days on end draped over a fence in plain view of the children inside the compound. The children must have suffered terrible visions because, reportedly, vultures and other beasts of prey devoured parts of his body (the man's distraught wife was also inside the compound). Reno's troops eventually sent in a helicopter that picked up the remains off the fence with a grappling hook and flew them away.

Finally, Janet Reno cared so much for the welfare of these desperate kids that she ordered tanks to ram and batter the walls of their home, puncturing holes in the structures, knocking the buildings off their foundations. This caused doors and windows to become stuck and inoperable, and stairways to collapse so that the children and adults could not escape the fiery holocaust soon to come.

Ms. Reno next directed her ATF and FBI storm troopers to pump CS gas into the building housing these children—a type of gas so virulent and harmful its use is outlawed in international conflicts by the Geneva Convention, an international treaty.[32]

Nazi dictator Adolf Hitler had refused in World War II to use chemical weapons against his opponents, even though the very fate of his nation and his own life were at stake. Yet, a hell-bent Janet Reno gave the green light to her hundreds of military forces camped outside the Branch Davidian complex to torment the men, women, *and children* with this chemical agent originally invented in the very pit of hell.

Chemical warfare experts have testified that CS gas, an inflammatory agent more lethal and insidious than the tear gas used by police in riot situations, should *never* be used in enclosed spaces—*a fire may result.*

CS gas is also known to produce these horrendous effects in its victims: burning eyes, severe nausea and vomiting, dizziness, unconsciousness, headaches, stomachaches, rashes, and mental confusion.[33]

Yes, Janet Reno, that's what *you did* to those children. Your savage gas attack and assault on their young bodies and minds lasted for six, hideously monstrous hours. You made their life a living hell until, finally, you roasted them to death.

Not satisfied with the torture and pain she had already inflicted on the kids inside the compound, I believe that, in spite of her statements to the contrary, Reno gave the order for the FBI and ATF to set the compound on fire—to mutilate and burn the kids alive. Evidently, federal sharpshooters and goon squads were also sent in prior to the fire to assassinate sect leader David Koresh and top lieutenants. They and over 20 other Koresh followers were found shot in the head, according to the official coroner's report.[34]

Targeted for Extermination

The Clinton/Reno message was made loud and clear: In the future there are at least *three reasons* why individuals or groups may be targeted by the Clintonistas for intimidation and, possibly, death:

(1) *Ownership of guns*: It doesn't matter if the firearms you own are legal because the Clintonistas want to disarm all Americans. Why? For purposes of government control.

(2) *Christian faith*: According to Bill Clinton and the femiNazis, any group that can even vaguely be described as "Christian fundamentalist" is not fit to exist. Such groups

are considered a threat to the New Age, New World Order. Especially hated and condemned are pseudo-Christian groups which claim to be "Israel" or "Jewish." The Koresh sect, for example, professed to be "Jewish," and came complete with a "Jewish Messiah" (Vernon Howell *aka* David Koresh) and a Jewish Star of David flag flying atop their compound. The Branch Davidians also observed Jewish High Holy Days.[35]

I believe it is significant that Attorney General Janet Reno, who is Jewish, was on the Board of Directors of the Jewish Anti-Defamation League (ADL).[36] The ADL, which has been accused of being a terrorist organization with ties to Israel's Mossad spy agency, is known to keep voluminous computer files on hundreds of organizations the group considers its enemies. Included are many reputable Christian and pro-life ministries and organizations. The ADL also employs private investigators to do its dirty work, and reportedly, some police officers in cities across the U.S.A. are covertly in its hire.

In 1992, the ADL's offices in San Francisco were raided by the police and their files were seized after a valid search warrant was obtained. Possible indictments against ADL officials are expected.

Documentation is also available that the ADL pressured the FBI and the federal government to take action against the Branch Davidians. In fact, Herb Brin, an ADL official, boasted in a Los Angeles area Jewish community publication, *Heritage*, "U.S. and Texas authorities have precise documentation (from the ADL of course) on the Branch Davidian cult in Texas."[37]

(3) *Race or Social Ideology*: The Clintonistas believe that white people especially, but also groups of all races and ethnic origins who wish to be *separatists*, must be dealt with harshly because they are a threat to the *multiculturalism* ideology. Muslims and Orthodox Jews, also because of their separatist beliefs, are despised by the Clintonistas. But in the case of the Orthodox Jewish groups, Clinton administration officials are unable to move against them because they fear the powerful Jewish lobby. This may change very soon.

Islamic groups are also a daunting target. Black Muslims in America are very militant and would fight back if attacked. They also have strong support from the African-American community and from the leaders of civil rights groups. Foreign-controlled Islamic groups based in America are an easier mark, especially if the feds can goad their radical leaders into perpetrating highly visible acts of terror such as the bombing of the New York World Trade Center. However, the persecution of such groups must be handled in a most delicate way so as not to upset the Arab and Moslem world community.

What's left, then, as the easiest marks are the Christian fundamentalists, the white separatists, and gun owner groups and individuals. Therefore, we can expect that more and more of these groups will suffer from Reno's propaganda squads, her black-hooded, SWAT team raids, and her murderous Gestapo attacks in the future.

The perfect candidate for Clintonista extermination is thus the Christian (or pseudo-Christian) fundamentalist group that owns guns and practices separatism. If children are available to be used as a pretext for the assault, so much the better.

Neo-Nazi skinhead groups, identity churches, America First organizations, and even solid, old-fashioned, Gospel-preaching churches and pastors are high up on the Clintonista agenda for police action. Even though these groups have widely divergent views, the Clinton people put them all in the same bushel basket.

Some may rejoice that groups with strange or unorthodox views and beliefs are the targets for persecution, but note this: Once these groups are snuffed out without a sizeable whimper of complaint from the citizenry at large, then all the others mentioned above will next be targeted.

Eventually, *anyone* and *everyone* who disagrees with the fascist regime in the White House might find themselves in dire jeopardy.

Yes, the bell may toll for you, too, in due time!

The Waco Massacre a Nazi Atrocity?

If identifying the Waco tragedy as a Nazi atrocity sounds
overly dramatic or sensationalist, please understand that
though the mass media generally refuse to give them a
hearing, there are many outstanding Americans concerned
about the implications of Janet Reno's unconstitutional assault
on the children and adults in Waco.

Respected national columnist Alexander Cockburn, author
of several highly acclaimed books and a contributor to *Nation*
and many other publications, wrote a column for the *Los
Angeles Times* in which he put the Clinton/Reno massacre in
the same category as the Salem witch hunts and the Nazi
atrocities of fascist Germany.[38] By labeling the Branch
Davidians a "cult," said Cockburn, Janet Reno, Bill Clinton,
and their heavily armed assault squads, claimed exemption
"from justice and compassion."[39]

Cockburn also roundly criticized Janet Reno's unfounded
propaganda claim that she had only done it to prevent child
abuse:

> To call someone a child abuser these days is like calling
> someone a communist in the 1950s or a witch in the 17th
> century. Normal standards of evidence or reason don't
> apply.

> There was compelling evidence, claimed President Clinton's
> spokesman George Stephanopoulos, that the children were
> being abused . . . In fact, the FBI has conceded that *there's
> no evidence for these chilling claims*. But child abuse is
> a headline grabber and conscience-absolver, as Reno knows
> well from her days as a prosecutor in Dade County.[40]

Alexander Cockburn's noteworthy, heavily documented
article then went on to recount several instances in which
Janet Reno, as a Miami, Florida prosecutor, had used
"children's rights" as a pretext for terrible abuse of judicial
restraint. Cockburn further noted that the "appalling event"

in Waco "took place on April 19, 1943, the 50th anniversary of the Nazi assault on the Jewish ghetto in Warsaw."[41]

Cockburn wrote that, "The Nazis, too, regarded cults as ripe candidates for persecution. On July 20, 1937, the SS Reichsfuhrer Reinhard Heydrich ordered the banning and persecution of small religious sects."[42]

What happened in Waco, says Cockburn, was "a saga of Nazi-like affront to religious tolerance." Worse, he writes, is that the "deprogrammers" of such unsavory groups as the Cult Awareness Network, who, early on, promoted the government attack on the Davidians, now want the Clinton administration's Janet Reno and her federal prosecutors to let them "exercise their dark arts on the burned Davidian survivors so that they testify correctly and desist from maintaining—as they have—that no mass suicide was under way."[43]

"Onward to Salem: gas, fire, and brainwashing, courtesy of the Justice Department,"[44] Cockburn admonished.

Ethnic Cleansing: A Vulgar Display

John Ed Pearce, writing in an Indiana newspaper, *The Courier-Journal,* branded the Reno atrocity as "Ethnic Cleansing: Texas Style."[45] Pearce sarcastically observed that the feds, who assaulted the Davidians with their tanks and assault rifles, felt they could not let David Koresh keep guns within his compound—not in a place like Texas, "where there are more than four guns to every citizen. It could give the place a bad name."[46]

Janet Reno, Pearce wrote, did not just sit idly by doing her knitting. She:

"... passed the word sternly: Gas em ... Get this over with. And President Clinton, after being informed of the lethal plans and nodding his approval, wallowed in sorrow, poor fellow, as the flames consumed the cultists (formerly humans). But that's what happens to fanatics, he warned (fanatics being people who believe deeply things the majority does not believe.)"[47]

Former Waco District Attorney Vic Fazell, who had arrested Koresh several years before the Reno massacre and tried him on state charges (of which Koresh was acquitted by a jury), commented that the siege by Reno and her federal agents "was a vulgar display of power. If they had simply phoned Koresh and talked to him on the phone," said Fazell, "the Davidians would have given them what they wanted."[48]

True, Koresh would have generously allowed the ATF to search his premises, for *there were no illegal weapons whatsoever in the compound*—no machine guns, no 50 caliber, no Stealth bombers or nuclear weapons. Just a few hundred, regular old rifles and firearms, the same types possessed by millions of other law-abiding Texans.

However, to merely search the premises was not what the feds wanted to do! Otherwise, they could have phoned Koresh and then went in *unarmed* to accomplish their work at the compound.

No, they *intended* to kill Koresh and his top people. That is why, early that morning, they went in with assault weapons blazing and helicopter gunships overhead firing high-caliber rounds straight through the roof, killing some women and children as they lay peacefully sleeping in bed. That is why they rehearsed and practiced the military-style assault for months on end.[49]

That is why the feds invited some of their friends in the news media to accompany them on their deadly raid. *The federal agents were convinced that Koresh and his people, reputed to be peaceful and friendly, would neither struggle nor return their murderous fire.* That is why the woman press agent of the ATF, immediately following the initial, failed assault, expressed shock and surprise. "We were outgunned," she said.[50]

Tragically, the tapes of this incident, even after some fancy editing by Janet Reno's storm trooper technicians back in their Washington, D.C., FBI labs, nevertheless still contain this revealing—and heart breaking statement. Koresh's voice is heard as he exclaims:

> You brought a bunch of guys out here and you killed some of my children. We told you we wanted to talk . . . I don't care who they are. Nobody is going to come to my home, with my babies around, shaking guns without a gun in their face. That's just not the American way.[51]

"That's Just Not the American Way"

"That's just not the American way," said David Koresh. What an indictment of the Nazis who raided his home and savagely murdered those poor children!" "That's just not the American way."

But it *is* the way of the future, as "pink beret" Janet Reno and the Clinton team consolidate their hold on America and become more and more audacious in their assaults on our liberties and our way of life.

As I write this, the government is preparing a "show trial" of the 12 remaining survivors of Reno and Clinton's Waco massacre. Stalin and Hitler also had their purges and their show trials of the innocent who had been selected out as examples to instill fear in the masses. If, as citizens, we do nothing to stop this horrible injustice, we are not deserving of the name "Americans."

Yes, dear reader, you and I *are* Americans, citizens of a great nation whose Constitution, abused by some in power, is still a living, breathing document guaranteeing individuals and groups of widely divergent views—Christians, the David Koreshes, atheists, Neo-Nazis, Jews, New Agers, Black Muslims, and others—freedom and liberty from government tyrants who would oppress them.

I believe that we must regain our moorings as a Christian nation; yet, as Christians, we do not discriminate nor do we persecute others. Moreover, if the government abuses one of us, it abuses all of us. Isn't it time, therefore, that we *act* like

Americans and peacefully, yet with courage and determination, put an end to this oppression?

M A R G A R E T R I C H A R D S O N

Position: IRS Commissioner

Moniker: *The Enforcer*

What a revolting development! Hillary's Yale University Law School classmate, Margaret Richardson, is now in charge of America's most feared, well-oiled police organization.[1] Armed with stunning law enforcement powers, the Internal Revenue Service easily has the ability to financially destroy any and all enemies of the Clinton White House.

What's worse, with impressive computer efficiency, the IRS has the awesome capability of scrutinizing millions of U.S. citizens, tracking the most minute details of their financial affairs and even the most intimate information about their private lives.

A Law Unto Itself

The New American magazine recently published a revealing—and scary—article about the IRS entitled, "A Law Unto Itself." The author noted that the agency has 123,000 employees—five times more than the FBI! In addition, the IRS "has independent authority to impose civil penalties and *no* legal obligation to take a person to court before seizing his car, home, paycheck, or other property."[2]

If the IRS chooses, it can turn its big guns on any person or organization chosen to be its target for demolition. "The massive size and staggering ambiguity of the IRS tax code makes nearly every taxpayer an almost certain lawbreaker," wrote *The New American.*

An IRS memorandum quoted in the March 1980, *Saturday Review* asserted: "Agents should be able to discover errors in 99.9 percent of all returns if they want."[3]

That was as far back as 1980. Imagine how much more this is true today, after about fifteen more years of increasingly complex and cumbersome new tax codes have been tacked on.

What this means is that any politically incorrect citizen can, at any time, be fingered for persecution, auditing, and investigation. Even the most honest person, who keeps the most meticulous of records, can be unfairly charged with criminal activity.

During the 30s the feds used "tax evasion" as an excuse to put away Al Capone and dozens of other bootleggers and hoods. Most Americans hollered out, "Bravo!" Now, in the 90s, if the White House and its gaggle of liberal Clintonistas choose to do so, they could unleash the IRS against an entire, new class of supposed "law breakers": conservative Americans and Christians who oppose Big Sister government. Everyone who opposes huge and onerous tax increases and a United Nations-centered New World Order could find themselves at risk. Opponents of special privileges for gays may also find themselves in the gun sights of the White House's politically correct SWAT teams.

Feeling the Heat

Conservative Christian churches and ministries, as well as patriotic, America First groups, organizations, and newsletters could also feel the heat of the IRS enforcers, egged on by

Hillary's Hellcats. Those with tax exempt status could be threatened with losing that status *unless* they moderate their rhetoric or, possibly, *join* the pro-Clinton, pro-New World Order propaganda bandwagon.

A precedent for this has already occurred. During the 1992 national elections, an evangelical church in Binghamton, New York, ran ads opposing Bill Clinton's support for homosexual rights, abortion, and distribution of condoms in public schools. The church ads asked, "Do we really want as a president and role model for our children a man of this character who supports this type of behavior?"[4]

Shortly after the election, the IRS launched an investigation of the church.

According to the IRS interpretation of the law, leaders of a church or tax exempt organization or group cannot involve themselves in partisan politics. The rub is that there is no precise definition of the term, "politics." Highly regarded, political theorist Harold Lasswell once defined politics as the art of determining "who gets what, when, and how." Obviously, this is such a hazy and amorphous definition that little can be established in the way of proper legal boundaries.

When a tax exempt church, using the Bible as its guide, publicly opposes pornography, gay special privileges, corruption in government, or violence on TV, is this a "political" stand? Or is the church's pastor simply taking a historically acceptable stand against religious and immoral degeneracy?

When a patriotic educational group favors keeping the U.S.A. a sovereign and independent republic rather than allowing its merger into a North American Free Trade Zone, is this really a politically *partisan* position? One would think not, but then again, ultimately, the IRS has the hammer—and the resources—to attempt to squelch free speech and activity opposed by White House overlords and their IRS Commissioner.

An Enemies List?

The Nixon White House developed an "Enemies List" and used the IRS as its bully boy to intimidate, harass, and shut down opposition. Have things, however, changed for the better since the wild and open 70s? Probably not. In 1986, a federal judge, ruling in favor of a couple who had been wrongly harmed by the fraudulent actions of the IRS, compared the agency to a "rogue elephant" stomping on the rights of honest American citizens.[5]

Given the fact that her Yale pal, Margaret Richardson, now sits in the catbird seat as IRS Commissioner, presiding over America's most fearsome and vast law enforcement apparatus, Hillary has the potential to do much harm. Unless Ms. Richardson surprises us with an unexpected display of integrity and fair play, bedraggled, conservative, Christian Americans may well find themselves persecuted and tortured by the very agency created back in 1913 by Woodrow Wilson and his superiors in the Secret Brotherhood to punish, control, and rob the masses: the Internal Revenue System.

ALICE RIVLIN

Position: Deputy Director, Office of Management and Budget

Moniker: *Ms. Bilderberg*

When the Clintons chose former U.S. Representative Leon Panetta as director of the most powerful financial agency in Washington, the Office of Management and Budget (OMB), it was just window dressing. Panetta is liked by his fellow congressmen, handles the media well, and, as titular head of OMB, is mainly in charge of public relations. The real power, however, lies with his chief deputy, Alice Rivlin.

It is Rivlin who "cooks the books." She's the day-to-day, master accountant and policy maven who insures that the Clintonista money plan is consistent with the goals set in advancing hidden elitists behind the scenes—the men whom I call the "Secret Brotherhood" in my book, *Dark Majesty*.

These men, unknown to the public at large, control the U.S. government primarily through their front group, the Council on Foreign Relations (CFR). The CFR has approximately 2,700 members, and both Bill Clinton and George Bush are part of this "distinguished" Jacobin network.

Rivlin: The CFR/Trilateral Connection

The CFR has only 25 directors, and Alice Rivlin is one of them. Indeed, there are only three women, including Rivlin, who hold a director's position.[1] As a director, Ms. Rivlin has undoubtedly been made privy to the most confidential plans of the CFR conspirators. In her previous post as the first director for the Congressional Budget Office (1975-1983), her task was to communicate to the leaders of Congress the financial wishes and desires of the CFR bigwigs and to oversee and coordinate the Congressional budget to guarantee that the dictates of the elitists were carried out.

In other words, as a member of the CFR's Board of Directors and through her influential position as head of the Congressional Budget Office, Alice Rivlin appears to have been a major conduit and link between the unelected power brokers of David Rockefeller's CFR and the U.S. Congress.

Ms. Rivlin evidently performed this same role for the exclusive *Bilderbergers* group. As explained in *Dark Majesty*, the Bilderbergers, founded in 1954, is made up of about 125 of the most wealthy and powerful men in the world, all of whom hail from either Europe or the United States. They meet privately at least once each year to plot out the world's economic future for the coming year.[2]

Only a handful of women have ever been invited to the inner sanctum of the mysterious Bilderbergers. But again, Alice Rivlin is proven to be a favored child of the New World Order set. She is also a Bilderberger, having secretly gone to several of their meetings, with her travel expenses paid for by taxpayer funds, courtesy of the U.S. Congress.[3] Rivlin's primary role in regards to the Bilderbergers was the same as it was for the CFR. She took notes and reported to the Bilderberg leadership the state of financial and political affairs in the U.S.A. and then dutifully reported to the leaders of Congress what the powerful Bilderbergers expected them to accomplish over the coming months.

Confirming Ms. Rivlin's role as the conduit of financial information between elected U.S. leaders and the leadership of private groups and secret societies who rule over us from behind the scenes, is her membership in two other important front groups—the Brookings Institute, a liberal think tank, and the Trilateral Commission (TLC).[4]

Her active involvement in such one worldism groups as the CFR, the TLC, the Bilderbergers, and the Brookings Institute stamps Alice Rivlin as the most loyal of servants of the globalist Secret Brotherhood. Now, as the Clinton's in-house budget manager, she is well placed to continue her valuable service to the hidden masters of international finance.

Unorthodox Economics

Like other socialists in high office in the Clintonista administration, Alice Rivlin is a woman with decidedly unorthodox economic philosophies—philosophies which, as R.E. McMaster notes in a recent issue of his financial and investment newsletter, *The Reaper*, "reveal her communist leanings." McMaster points especially to Rivlin's praise for *"centrally planned economies"* and her desire to *"provide lifetime security for workers."* [5]

Another of Rivlin's socialist ideas should strike fear in the hearts of every red-blooded American taxpayer: She is on record as advocating the centralizing of all property taxes under the control of federal bureaucrats in Washington, D.C. [6]

Understandably, patriotic Americans are alarmed over the potential damage she may do to the nation's economy and future. "Alice Rivlin," Fritz Springmeier warns, "is a communist of the worst economic type. Her book, *Reviving The American Dream*, calls for centrally planned economies." [7]

As deputy budget director for the Clintons, Alice Rivlin should feel right at home. Her White House, feminist counterpart, Laura D'Andrea Tyson, chairman of the Council of Economic Advisors, is also a fan of centrally planned economies—such as the ones imposed on slave populations by communist dictators like Russia's Joseph Stalin and Romania's Nikolai Ceausescu.

DONNA SHALALA

Position: Secretary of Health and Human Services

Moniker: *The High Priestess of Political Correctness*

"**D**onna Shalala, *you know* you're a lesbian, and *we know* you're a lesbian. So why don't you just come out of the closet and admit it?" These are words of homosexual firebrand Larry Kramer, co-founder of the gay activist group, ACT-

UP, who "outed" Donna Shalala over national television in April of 1993.[1] The occasion was the homosexual/lesbian march in Washington, a mega-event attended by approximately 350,000 gay men and women demanding special privileges and affirmative action for their kind.

Designated an official "Friend of Hillary" (FOH) by *Newsweek* magazine, Shalala is a *real* liberal.[2] In fact, she's so proud of the label that she's openly bragged about it. Shalala has also earned a notorious, but well-deserved, reputation as one of the meanest and most diabolically militant *Christian haters* in America today.

Shalala has rightly been called the "High Priestess of Political Correctness," a title richly earned due to her anti-Christian persecution of so-called "politically" and "religiously incorrect" students at the University of Wisconsin where Shalala held leadership as chancellor.[3]

Her Nazi-Inspired "Hate Speech" Code

As chancellor, Donna Shalala made it one of her prime goals to drive true Christian believers off the campus. In a Nazi, police state type campaign to intimidate and shut Christians up, she originated what she called her "hate speech" code. Joined by other liberal ideologues on the university's board of regents, Shalala drafted rules that banned the use of any language, epithets, or symbols which "demean" a person or group because of race, religion, gender, ancestry, age, disability, or sexual preference.[4]

New Agers, pedophiles, sexually kinky types (the leather and chains, sadist crowd), satanists, occultists, homosexuals and lesbians, multiculturals, and other one worlders, as well as strangely nontraditional staff, faculty, students, and hangers-on, were delighted. Shalala's new University of Wisconsin hate crimes ordinance meant that the Christians on campus, espousing their detestable, "Jesus is the *only way* to salvation" philosophy, could finally be silenced once and for all. To claim that *your* religion is better or more true than someone else's—now *that's* pure hate, they reasoned.

Sure enough, complaints based on what was called "The Madison Plan" began to be filed against Christian students and professors who favorably commented on traditional moral values. To express one's opinion that Buddhism, Witchcraft, or Islam is not valid was adjudged "hate speech." To say that a woman's place is in the home also was deemed "hate speech." To assert that blacks and other racial minorities should receive equal treatment under the law rather than preferential quotas in jobs, etc.—that, too, was said to be "hate speech."[5]

Especially categorized a hate crime according to Shalala and many of her gestapo bosom buddies, was any opinion or comment that reflected negatively on homosexuality and lesbianism as less than a perfectly wonderful, even positive and wholesome, lifestyle. "Homophobia," as the new cadre of Himmler's ghost labeled the "mental disease" which evidently afflicts a majority of American citizens, would not be tolerated on the *"thought cleansed"* campus of the University of Wisconsin.

Religious Cleansing to Insure Multiculturalism

Connie Zhu, reporting in *The Christian American* newspaper, correctly charged that Shalala's "Madison Plan" was "a politically correct program which advocated hiring minority faculty and admitting minority students in keeping with her goal of implementing a multicultural approach to education."[6]

According to an April 1992 article in *Heterodoxy*, "Academic integrity was always secondary to Shalala's numbers game." While she was chancellor of the University of Wisconsin at Madison, its academic reputation slipped. This was because she "subordinated every other aspect of life at the university to the success of what she called *multiculturalsim*." Under the plan, deans of the wrong color and/or gender were replaced.[7]

In other words, Donna Shalala proved herself to be a racist bigot who discriminated against people who were of the "wrong" color or sex. Shalala turned out, then, to be the biggest hater of humanity who ever held a top university post in the United States. The worst redneck professor at the University of Alabama or at Georgia State during the racially bitter 1960s could not compare to this woman so full of hatred and venom for the classes of people whom she believes inferior—whites, American Christians, and men.

Star Chambers of Shalala's Nazi "Thought Police"

During her administration from 1988 to 1993, many "incorrect thinking" people were hauled up before the star chambers of Donna Shalala's University of Wisconsin insane asylum to answer charges of "hate speech." Richard Long, an art professor, who had been on the Madison, Wisconsin campus for 22 years, was one of them. Long says he had seen the academic atmosphere change drastically during the five years of Shalala's administration, but he had no idea that he, himself, would get caught up in Donna Shalala's ever-widening dragnet.[8]

Long was accused of everything in the book. It was "informally" reported that he "might have" made remarks that were "unfriendly" to minorities, women, and homosexuals.

"I never had the chance to produce witnesses on my behalf," says Long, "and I was never confronted formally with the charges." Long insisted that he had never knowingly offended anyone.

Although the U.S. Constitution forbids a citizen from being tried for crimes without a grand jury indictment and a fair and impartial trial by his or her peers, Long and others like him who were falsely accused by Shalala's university, hate crimes patrol, were never afforded these rights. Nor were Long and some of the others given an opportunity to confront their accusers, yet another constitutional right.

Nevertheless, for those convicted by the hate tribunals

of universities such as Wisconsin, punishments meted out can be devastating. Professors and staff can be denied promotions and unceremoniously fired from their jobs. Their careers can be shattered, their reputations scarred, their lives destroyed.

In Professor Long's case, these dread consequences were averted when, after being forced to defend himself of unsubstantiated, hocus-pocus charges and after an agonizing period of uncertainty in his life, Long was found not guilty. Still, Richard Long says that the unfounded allegations continue to hang like a cloud over his now, quite tarnished reputation.[9]

This was how Donna Shalala, the High Priestess of Political Correctness, rewarded a man, Richard Long, who had built up a sterling record of 22 years of meritorious achievement at the University of Wisconsin.

A few brave souls did try to challenge Donna Shalala's "hate speech" code as an infringement on people's First Amendment rights to free speech, but Shalala stubbornly continued to implement the dreadnaught and draconian measure. The campus must be *cleansed*, her liberal supporters explained.

She Outliberals the Liberals

Astonishingly, the organization which finally succeeded in making Shalala and her activist, lesbian storm troopers sit up and take notice turned out to be the ultra-liberal American Civil Liberties Union (ACLU). Apparently, Ms. Shalala's absurd, mean-spirited, hate speech code was so outrageously unfair and so patently unconstitutional an affront that even the ACLU couldn't stomach any more of it.

So the ACLU challenged their liberal colleague's unseemly code in federal court, contending its provisions were "a restraint on free speech." The court ruled in the ACLU's favor and struck down Shalala's prohibitions in 1991.[10]

An angry, but undeterred and unrepentant Donna Shalala

immediately lashed back with fury, convening her university's law professors, directing them to rewrite the code to "make it valid." To make it easier to accomplish, Shalala conveniently misinterpreted the court's ruling, erroneously claiming that it was still okay to prohibit hate speech that is "intentional." In other words, she had her lawyers—at taxpayer's expense naturally, since the University of Wisconsin is a state-supported institution—draw up new rules that say hate speech is only permissible if it is "accidental." If the person, however, *meant* to say it, the speech remains a hate crime.[11]

This means, for example, that a student who is a Christian is still risking sanctions for the "offense" of *intentionally* telling a fellow student about the Gospel message—that Jesus is Lord.

Only Christians and Patriots Targeted

Isn't it peculiar that except for a few "skinhead" and other fringe groups, only Christians and conservative, patriotic Americans are punished for "hate crimes?" Atheists, New Agers, feminist radicals and followers of Wicca, who frequently curse Christian fundamentalists and falsely berate and accuse conservatives of the most heinous things, are winked at. Frequently, such groups and individuals are applauded and praised for their hate speech.

Christian bashing and the ridicule of Americans with traditional values are the two most popular sports on university campuses these days, thanks to bigots like Donna Shalala and her liberal henchmen (or is it henchwomen?).

If Christian and American traditionalist bashing were an Olympic sport, there could be little doubt that Donna Shalala would easily win the coveted gold medal. As I've shown, Shalala has demonstrated that she's so radically liberal, she outliberals the liberal ACLU.

It is wise to consider the strong possibility that Shalala will use her high position at HHS to duplicate for the entire nation the damage she wreaked during her tenure as university chancellor. Interestingly, an editorial in Israel's respected *The Jerusalem Post* newspaper, mentioned Shalala as a prime example of how the Clintons are seeding the U.S. with "warmed-over remnants of the Carter administration— officials who ran one of the most miserable and unsuccessful administrations of the century." The newspaper gave this insightful illustration:

> Clinton's Secretary of Health and Human Services is Donna Shalala, Chancellor of the University of Wisconsin in Madison. She is a leading advocate of "political correctness"—that insidious form of thought control masquerading as liberalism and egalitarianism.[12]

Odious Fascism Chills Free Speech

Across America, "literally hundreds of universities have adopted (hate) speech codes," says Charles Sykes, a senior fellow at the Wisconsin Policy Research Institute.[13] These disgusting unAmerican restrictions on the right of free speech have become all the vogue during the last decade. The United States somehow got along and even prospered for over 200 years without such odious, fascist-like limits on speech. But if Hillary's Hellcats get their way, Americans will never again be free to state their opinions and reveal their innermost thoughts and musings.

How proud Adolf Hitler would be if he could only be alive today to see how the philosophies of his national socialist (Nazi) party have finally been adopted and promoted with newly enthused vigor by his modern disciples—Hillary Rodham Clinton, Donna Shalala, Patricia Achtenberg, *et al*.

Richard Long, the art professor who discovered first hand just how shrewdly evil and cunning the despicable doctrines of the femiNazi Hellcats can be, once was quoted as exclaiming (of Shalala's strong arm, Hitlerite tactics): "Was that McCarthyism, or what?"[14]

No, Professor Long, what has happened to you and

thousands of other innocent Americans caught up in the nets of the new *thought police* has nothing to do with McCarthyism. The late Senator Joseph McCarthy, who represented the voters of Wisconsin in the U.S. Congress, would not have allowed such gestapo tactics to prevail at a public university in his state.

What is happening now was not learned from the honorable Joseph McCarthy, a man whom history has fully vindicated. These are policies and tactics that come from the tattered and bloodstained files of Joseph Stalin, Joseph Goebbels, and Mao Tse Tung. They deserve no place in American society; they are a disgrace to the very founders of this once great nation. Sadly, we can only expect more of the same from the Hillary and Bill bunch. We can, that is, until Americans begin to stand up for their rights and put a stop to such injustices.

No Love for America or Christianity

The awful truth is that Shalala and the other "Friends of Hillary" are America haters, who have no love for this nation's most cherished traditions and no respect for its constitution. Their goal for America is a multicultural society devoid of Christian values but infused with Eastern religious philosophy and Wiccan theology. This is why *Heterodoxy* reports that at the University of Wisconsin, "courses like Buddhist theology and Hindu mysticism that had a dozen or so students before Shalala's arrival, now have ten times that many."[15]

Christians at Shalala's institution, fearing repercussions and dismissal, were forced to go underground. But anarchists, homosexuals and lesbian activists were encouraged to run rampant on campus. In 1991, lesbian students protesting the presence of armed forces ROTC at the university interrupted a board of regents meeting with shouts and physical demonstrations. They then began a public display of homosexual kissing and hugging. Were they ejected? Not on your life. Later, Shalala announced that she would meet with a senior Pentagon official to present the students' demands that the military's ban on homosexuals be ended.[16]

Imagine what would have happened if *Christian* students had interrupted that regents meeting, clapping their hands and singing gospel hymns! You know and I know that Donna Shalala would have instantly had the university police wrestle them to the floor, put handcuffs on their wrists, and brutally herd the students into waiting paddy wagons. Within 24 hours of their release from jail, Shalala would have had them pack their bags.

The New Brown Shirts

Increasingly, due to the criminally monstrous actions of Shalala and friends, America is developing a Gestapo mentality. In Hitler's Nazi Germany the brown shirts roamed the streets, grabbing newspapers whose writings they disagreed with from street vendors and destroying entire press runs. The brown shirts falsely accused Jews and others of crimes of which the accused were not guilty.

Now consider an incident that happened recently at the University of Pennsylvania, a school whose president is an old liberal chum of Bill and Hillary's. When Gregory Paulik, an engineering student, wrote a political commentary in the campus newspaper, criticizing laws that discriminate against whites and admission standards that give preference to blacks, anarchist black and minority students on campus flew into a violent rage.

One group, calling itself "The Working Committee of Concerned Black and Latino Students," confiscated *all* of the 14,000 copies of that day's *Daily Pennsylvanian* and threw them into dumpsters and trash cans. A spokesperson for the group said they were protesting the "blatant racism" evidenced by Paulik's column.[17]

The university not only *did not* punish this outrageous, fascist attack against a free press, university officials applauded it. Under pressure from the administration, the *Daily Pennsylvanian* was forced to publish a letter from African-American students and faculty severely condemning the staff of the newspaper for being without "a sliver of morality."[18]

Hillary and Bill Clinton and their Nazi cronies were so impressed with the way that Sheldon Hackney, the president of the University of Pennsylvania, handled this matter that only a month later, the Clintons appointed Hackney to become executive director of the National Endowment for the Humanities.[19]

What difference is there, if any, between the fascists at the universities of Wisconsin and Pennsylvania and their predecessors who once savaged hapless innocents on the streets of Munich and Berlin?

Constitutional Rights in Jeopardy

Our constitutional rights are being gravely jeopardized by Hillary's Hellcats. Indeed, they are being completely ignored by the new totalitarians. How wise were our nation's founders who warned that if America's Christian values were ever diminished or cast aside, not even a written constitution with its supposed guarantees of liberty and freedom would protect the citizenry:

> Only a virtuous people are capable of freedom. As nations become corrupt and vicious, they have more need of masters.
>
> —Benjamin Franklin

> Neither the wisest constitution nor the wisest laws will secure the liberty and happiness of a people whose manners are universally corrupt.
>
> —Samuel Adams

Shalala Surveys Her Vast Kingdom

From her imperial throne—her seat as head of the federal government's mammoth-sized Department of Health and Human Services (HHS)—Shalala can survey a vast, feudalistic system over which she reigns as High Priestess. The fiscal year budget for HHS now tops $590 billion; more money is spent here than at any other agency, including the defense department. HHS employs 126,000 people—more people than live in a medium size U.S. city. As its administrator, Shalala presides over the Social Security system, the Public Health Service, the Food and Drug Administration, the National Institutes of Health, the Office of Consumer Affairs, AIDS programs, Medicare, Medicaid, the Head Start educational program, the welfare system, and the list continues.

How awful to have an unAmerican and anti-Christian bigot in control of such massive bureaucratic powers!

Franklin Sanders, publisher of *The Moneychanger,* is just one of many astute political and spiritual commentators who have issued warnings about the neo-Nazi leanings of Ms. Shalala:

> She's been warehoused by the establishment for a long, long time, in the CFR, TLC, and on the board of the ILE, among other places. She was the champion of *political correctness* as Chancellor at the University of Wisconsin, helping to make thought and speech nazism a way of life there . . . In the Carter administration she was assistant secretary of Housing and Urban Development, the agency responsible for demolishing the hearts of most American cities. She will be in charge of the radical socialization of the American family, home, and child.[20]

Is Sanders correct? Is Donna Shalala, longtime bosom buddy of Hillary and a member in good standing of both the Council on Foreign Relations and the Trilateral Commission, now "in charge of the radical socialization of the American family, home, and child?"

A Vision of a Radical New America

Read this excerpt from an actual speech given by Shalala at the University of Chicago on November 15, 1991, and any doubts as to her unswerving devotion to ridding America of all remaining vestiges of its Christian heritage and destroying the traditional family will be quickly dissolved. In her speech, Shalala spelled out her utopian "vision" of how life should be for a typical child, by the name of "Renata," in America in the year 2004. This would be a decade after the Hillbillary administration has begun its redemptive work of *multicultural transformation*:

> Renata doesn't know any moms who don't work, but she knows lots of moms who are single. She knows some children who only live with their dads, and children who have two dads, or live with their mothers and their grandmothers. In her school books there are lots of different kinds of friends and families.
>
> After school, Renata goes to a daycare center operated by a neighbor who takes care of five children in her home. The back yard of the home is a playground which has been constructed with grant money from the city.
>
> At Thanksgiving time, Renata's teacher will tell a story about how people from Europe came to the United States, where the Indians lived. "She will say, 'It was just the same as if someone had come into your yard and taken all your toys and told you they weren't yours anymore."
>
> Renata will think of herself as being part of the world— not just her town or the United States. This will all happen because we made it our top priority in our communities and in our Congress.[21]

Shalala the Globalist Conspirator

Donna Shalala is one of only a handful of women who have been accepted into the sacrosanct, ivory tower ranks of the Council on Foreign Relations and the Trilateral Commission. This stamps her as a bonafide and doctrinaire New World Order ideologue who can be relied upon to push the tainted agenda of the super rich.[22]

Evidently, she has been made head of the federal government's largest agency for a special reason: to decimate the family and soften up America to be merged into a globalist, multicultural society. The tools she is to use include political correctness, radical feminism, "children's rights," revisionist history, class and race division, and the promotion of sodomites and the sodomite agenda throughout society.

The object of all this is *control*, and the Shalala/Hillary team is already on its way to achieving this key objective. One way, curiously enough, is to use health programs to implement control over the masses. Shalala wants the government to fund a universal immunization program for kids. Why? To save lives? No way. The real purpose is exposed by Shalala's insistence that the federal immunization program will include the requirement for every child, as an infant, to be *registered* with a new government bureau! National registration, i.e., *control*.

As head of HHS, Shalala is also working closely with Hillary on the proposed new, national health care package. The stated goal is to insure that *every American* be entered into the program to receive either free medical care or care provided mainly at the expense of employers. But there's a catch: as part of the program, each person will be required to apply for and be issued a *national identification card*. Again, we discover the true purpose—the government's ability to identify and track its citizens. We're talking about Big Sister again. Orwellian *Control*.

The Final Solution: Sucking Out the Brains of Babies

One of the scariest dimensions of Donna Shalala sitting on the throne at the Department of Health and Human Services involves the *abortion issue*—the tragedy of millions of babies slaughtered each year in abortuaries. Donna Shalala, like her mentor Hillary Rodham Clinton, is an *abortaholic*. They both need to attend a 12-step program to "kick the habit" of their torture and killing of innocent babies.

Now that Bill Clinton, at the urging and insistence of Hillary and Hillary's private secretary, Susan Thomases, has lifted the Reagan-Bush ban on the use of *fetal tissue* obtained from the brains and body parts of *aborted, live babies*, a bizarre new way of killing these infants has now come to America. As grotesque and inhumane as it is, the best way one can describe this heinous new abortion technique is to say that it involves the *sucking out of the brains of babies! Late term, fully developed babies!*

In *National Right to Life News*, Dr. Richard Glascow, the National Right to Life organization's education director, described this vampire-like procedure. Read his words . . . and greive:

> A gruesome, relatively new abortion technique is now being used to kill second—and third—trimester unborn babies by removing the baby's entire body, except for the head, and then sucking out her brains. The ghastly new technique, dubbed "D & X," was described in detail by Dr. Martin Haskell at a September 13, 1992, "Risk Management Seminar" sponsored by the National Abortion Federation, the trade association of the largest abortion facilities in the country.

> Because the opening of the woman's cervix must be greatly enlarged, a D & X abortion requires three days. The first two days are used to dilate the woman's cervix through the use of laminaria. These are cylindrical shaped or tapered devices which are inserted into the cervix and which gradually increase in diameter as they absorb water.

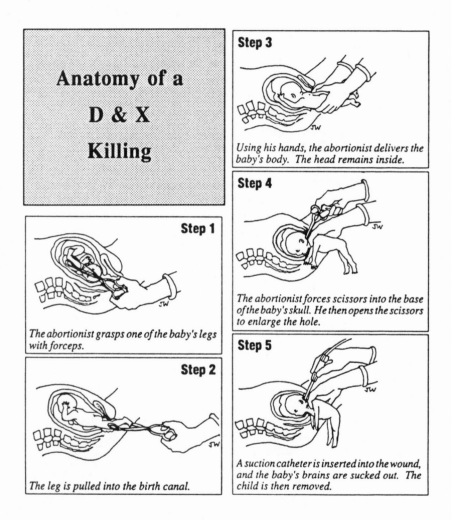

Anatomy of a D & X Killing

Step 1

The abortionist grasps one of the baby's legs with forceps.

Step 2

The leg is pulled into the birth canal.

Step 3

Using his hands, the abortionist delivers the baby's body. The head remains inside.

Step 4

The abortionist forces scissors into the base of the baby's skull. He then opens the scissors to enlarge the hole.

Step 5

A suction catheter is inserted into the wound, and the baby's brains are sucked out. The child is then removed.

The grim new techonology used in the killing of babies by abortionists called D & X allows abortion clinics to abort children up to 32 weeks or more. One American doctor, as of 1993, had already performed over 700 D & X abortions.

During the abortion procedure itself, Haskell initially uses ultrasound to identify how the unborn child is oriented in the uterus. Having located an "extremity," he inserts a forceps through the vagina and cervical canal into the uterus and grasps one of the baby's legs.

Having turned the unborn baby inside of the uterus so that she is oriented feet first and face down toward the floor, Haskell then pulls one of the child's legs out, then the other leg and the rest of the torso up to the child's neck. The baby is oriented spine up.

At this point, all of the baby's body is outside of the uterus except for the head, which is "usually" too large to pass through the cervix. At this point, in all likelihood the baby is still alive.

Sliding his hand up the baby's backbone, Haskell hooks his index and ring fingers over the shoulders and uses his middle finger to hold the woman's cervix away from the baby's neck. He then takes a pair of blunt-tipped surgical scissors, and after locating the base of the baby's skull, jams the scissors into the skull.

He spread the tips apart to enlarge the wound. After removing the scissors, Haskell inserts a suction catheter into the baby's skull and sucks out the brain, which he describes as "evacuating the skull's contents."

After the brain collapses, it is small enough to be removed through the cervix. Finally, Haskell removes the placenta with forceps and scrapes the uterine walls. The "procedure" is done. The baby's brains are then injected into patients who have Parkinson's disease.[23]

Nazi Doctors in America?

Anyone who has studied the accounts of Nazi doctors who performed their repugnant medical experiments and sacrilegious medical operations on doomed concentration camp inmates, understands exactly what is at stake with these new abortion procedures.

It was alleged that the Nazis used the body parts of their victims for commercial purposes. Now, a half century later, we seem to have learned almost nothing from past history. Today, in the gloriously dawning, radiant New Age of Hillary and her Hellcats, once again we violate the bodies of live human beings for a profit. Only this time we first suck out their brains!

My god! Has it come to this?

LAURA D'ANDREA TYSON

Position: Chairman of the Council of Economic Advisors

Moniker: *Comrade Commissar*

A communist in the White House? I'm afraid so. Maybe *worse* than a communist!

Laura D'Andrea Tyson is married to a man whose last name is Tarloff. But, as Franklin Sanders wryly notes, "Madame Tarloff, in keeping with the *femiNazi* practice, eschews (i.e., rejects) use of her husband's surname. Sanders warns that whether named Tyson, which she prefers, or Tarloff, the woman who now is chairman of the Council of

Economic Advisors possesses awesome powers that can minutely affect our pocketbooks and our daily lives. He predicts that, as one of the White House's top economic movers, Ms. Tyson will "push for fascism under the euphemism of *industrial policy.*"[1]

Hitler, of course, also was a strong advocate of a unique brand of government-controlled capitalism. He, too, believed in central management by bureaucrats and a *national industrial policy.* His economic philosophies were called fascism, or national socialism (Nazism).

However, Tyson's economic philosophy for America can probably best be described as *CommuNazi,* that is, a combination of communism and fascism. Her preference and predilection is for communism, but since that ultimate goal cannot be attained overnight, Comrade Tyson is willing *for now* to settle for fascism—an economy made up mostly of capitalist enterprises allowed to operate and make a profit, but forced to grovel before government overlords who can put them out of business at whim.

Laura Tyson, you see, is a former University of California at Berkeley radical. She's so radical that even the old communist, hard-line butcher Joseph Stalin might be proud. The American public has not been told the truth about this tyrannical economist's agenda for America, but the few brave men who've had the courage to investigate and expose what she stands for have been appalled and disgusted.

Tyson A Stalinist?

"This is a real winner!" Dr. Charles Provan remarked of Laura Tyson in his *American Freedom Movement* newsletter. "She supports communist central planning! She supported the Romanian socialism of Nikolai Ceausescu! This was the WORST economy in the former Eastern Bloc. She said, 'Did the Romanian investment plan work? Yes!' Tyson even admits that the Ceausescu plan 'conformed to the traditional Stalinist model.' "[2]

"The truth of the Romanian plan," Provan continued, "is that Ceausescu built a giant palance for himself and supplied perks for the Communist Party while the people had no food, no heat, no electricity and no medical care. This plan brought only poverty and death to Romania."[3]

Fritz Springmeier, a Christian researcher based in Oregon, believes that Laura Tyson's appointment to her high post is a convincing sign that the elite planners of the New World Order have, as their primary goal, the "financial control of the world by destruction of the economy." The plan, he writes, is to "move the American economy toward dictatorial socialism in preparation for a global, united economy."[4]

Laura Tyson's appointment as Chairman of the Council of Economic Advisors is, Springmeier believes, a major step toward fulfillment of this dark plot:

> Many of Clinton's top economic people are dyed-in-the-wool communists . . . Laura D'Andrea Tyson, head of Clinton's Council of Economic Advisors, has had only praise for the economic methods of Ceausescu and Stalin. Read her book, *Economic Adjustment in Eastern Europe*, if you want to be nauseated by her praise of the economic moves of those socialist dictators.[5]

Taxation Equals Control

To achieve their dictatorial socialist objectives, Hillary and Bill, urged on by their super-rich backers in America's unelected shadow government (see my revealing book, *Dark Majesty*), have a mighty weapon in the ability to tax the American public literally into oblivion. *Taxation equals control*, and the American people's capital and resources are now being transferred to Washington, D.C. at an unbelievably rapid rate.

In Laura Tyson, the Clintons and their henchmen have a powerful ally who favors more and more taxes. In order to appease a citizenry increasingly angry and rebellious over higher and higher taxes, Tyson has feigned "worry and concern" over growing federal deficits and has suggested that more taxes are the only solution.[6] Tyson and other fiscal liberals cannot imagine *cutting spending* to lower deficits. That, for them, would be unthinkable.

The *Wall Street Journal* commented recently on Laura Tyson's penchant for imposing ever increasing taxes on an already suffering and overtaxed citizenry:

> Taxes to the Horizon . . . Laura Tyson, head of the Administration's Council of Economic Advisors, has caught the Stockman Syndrome. David Stockman, the former Reagan OMB director, once talked about "deficits as far as the eye can see." Now along comes Ms. Tyson, predicting taxes as far as the eye can see. In a speech yesterday, she worried about the prospect of higher outlays for health down the road and raised the possibility of pursuing more deficit reduction after 1997 with consumption taxes or estate taxes. Ms. Tyson can peddle taxes all she wants, but we don't think she'll ever reach that horizon.[7]

How fascinating that Laura D'Andrea Tyson, as proven by the above quote, has let the cat out of the bag by telling us that the money to be spent for Hillary's health insurance scheme will cause much higher, government budget deficits. But not to worry! After 1997 (that would be *after* the Clintons win re-election), those higher deficits can be taken care of by cramming even more taxes down the people's throats. "Consumption taxes," for example, would include a national sales tax.

Tax Americans as hard as possible. That's the plan, because taxes equal Big Sister government. Big Sister government equals a combination of communism and fascism. That's CommuNazism, which equals totalitarianism. And that means control. Dictatorial control.

Stalin and his communist party had dictatorial control in Russia. Ceausescu and his socio-fascist gestapo had it in Romania. Someday very soon, if the Clintonistas succeed, we too, will have it right here in America. No wonder Laura

Tyson, the woman who has praised the economies of Stalin and Ceausescu, was chosen by the Hillbillary administration for her high position as overseer of the U.S. economy.

SHEILA WIDNALL

Position: Secretary of the Air Force

Moniker: *Rocket Lady*

"Off we go into the wild blue yonder . . ." Sheila Windnall is to become the first woman to head a branch of the U.S. Armed forces. (Where, oh where, is General Curtis LeMay when we need him *so* bad!) Actually, it appears that Professor Widnall, an aeronautical engineer with a doctorate from MIT, may really have many of the qualifications requisite for the job. Much of her research has been Air Force-oriented and she's been an avid supporter of air power.[1]

Widnall has served on the U.S. Air Force Academy's board of visitors and as an advisor to Wright-Patterson Air Force Base in Ohio.

However, being filthy rich and a Democrat didn't harm Widnall's chances of becoming Secretary of the Air Force, either. She's married to the affluent William Widnall, the son of a New Jersey congressman, who's been criticized for his membership in a yacht club which allegedly discriminates against minorities.[2]

Reportedly a heterosexual (she has two grown adult children), Sheila Widnall may find herself in a minority in more ways than one. In her new Pentagon post, she's a female leader immersed among the many men of the Air Force. At the same time, poor Sheila is evidently one of the few straight women in a sea of Clintonista gay appointees filling cabinet and other high-level positions. She'll, therefore, be *twice* a minority.

Footnotes and References

Part One   Now Let Us Praise Big Sister

1. Hillary Clinton, "People Who Inspire Me," *Parade*, April 11, 1993.

2. George Orwell, *1984* (New York: New American Library/Signet paperback edition, 1983; originally published with copyright 1949), p. 5.

3. *Ibid.*, p. 220.

4. *Ibid.*, p. 177.

5. *Ibid.*, p. 245.

6. "Sixty Years of Women We Love," *Esquire*, August, 1993.

7. Dan Rather quoted by Karen Sandstrom, "Rather Sees Change With Iraq," *Cleveland Plain Dealer*, January 15, 1993.

8. *The Reaper* (Address: P.O. Box 84901, Phoenix, AZ 85071), April 27, 1993, p. 4.

9. *Newsweek*, July 26, 1993, p. 3.

Part Two   Hillary Plays Hardball

1. *Vanity Fair*, September 1993.

2. Hillary Clinton, quoted by Floyd Brown, *Slick Willie* (Annapolis, Maryland: Annapolis Publishing Company, 1992, p. 70.

3. *Newsweek*, Winter/Spring 1993.

4. Jeffrey Gleckel, quoted by Robert Levin, *Bill Clinton: The Inside Story* (New York: SPI Books, 1992), pp. 90-91.

5. *Ibid.*

6. Bill Clinton, quoted in *Sunday Telegraph* (London) article, reprinted in *Washington Times*, May 2, 1993, p. A1.

7. Hillary Clinton, quoted by Floyd G. Brown, *Slick Willie* (Annapolis, Maryland: Annapolis Publishing Company, 1992), p. 73.

8. R.E. McMaster, *The Reaper*, July 20, 1993.

9. *Sunday Telegraph* (See footnote number 6 above).

10. *Time*, January 4, 1993, p. 41; and *Time*, May 10, 1993.

11. *Ibid.*

12. *Time*, May 10, 1993, p. 34.

13. *Ibid.*

14. *Ibid.*, p. 35.

15. *Ibid.*, p. 37.

16. Gary Blonston "Hillary's New Job Likely to Raise Controversy," *Knight-Ridder Newspapers*, January 25, 1993. Also see Eleanor Clift, "On the Road to Power...Hillary Is the Real Story, *Newsweek*, February 1, 1993, p. 38.

17. Judith Warner, *Hillary Clinton: The Inside Story* (New York: New American Library, paperback, 1993).

18. *Ibid.*, p. 155.

19. *Ibid.*

20. Jim Moore, *Clinton: Young Man In a Hurry* (Fort Worth, Texas: The Summit Group, 1992), p. 190.

21. Floyd G. Brown, *Slick Willie*, p. 70.

22. *Newsweek*, November 16, 1992, p. 42.

23. Albert R. Hunt, *Wall Street Journal*, January 19, 1993.

24. Larry Patterson, *Criminal Politics* (Address: P.O. Box 37432, Cincinatti, Ohio 45222), February 1993, p. 34.
25. *Ibid.*
26. Eleanor Clift, "Hillary's Ultimate Juggling Act," *Newsweek*, November 16, 1992.
27. *Sunday Telegraph, op. cit.*
28. *Newsweek*, November 16, 1992, p. 37.
29. This story and many that are similar have been reported in numerous publications. For example, see *The Reaper*, April 27, 1993, p. 4.
30. *The Reaper*, April 27, 1993, p. 4.
31. *Ibid.*
32. *Newsweek*, June 28, 1993, p. 17.
33. *Newsweek*, August 9, 1993, p. 15.
34. "Battle Scars," *Newsweek*, February 8, 1993.
35. Judith Warner, *op. cit.*, p. 201.

Part Three   Rage of the Psychopaths

1. Reprinted in *End Times and Victorious Living*, June/July, 1993, p. 9.
2. This allegation was broadcast over C-Span and discussed on the *Rush Limbaugh Show*.
3. Jack Wheeler, *Strategic Investment*, February 10, 1993.
4. "President Bill Clinton's Praise for Homosexuals and Lesbians Documents His Immoral Position," *Foundation*, January-February 1993, p. 31. Also see *San Francisco Chronicle*, November 14, 1992.
5. *Human Events*, June 26, 1993.
6. *Secret: FBI Documents Link Bill and Hillary Clinton to Marxist-Terrorist Network* (report available for $5 per copy plus postage) Sunset Research Group, 608 N. West Street, #236, Wichita, Kansas 67203. Also see *Insight*, September 28, 1992.
7. *Ibid.*
8. *Ibid.*
9. *Ibid.*
10. "Clinton's Communist Cluster Coordinator," *Christian American*, March 1993, p. 12. Also see Charles A. Provan, *The American Freedom Movement* newsletter (Address: The American Freedom Movement, P.O. Box 309, Irwin, PA 15642), 1993. Also reported in the *Washington Times, Washington Post, Atlanta Journal*, and *New York Times*.
11. *Ibid.*
12. Charles Provan, *Ibid.* Also see *Insight*, September 28, 1992, p. 4.
13. Thomas R. Eddlem, "Marxist Hillary?," *The New American*, August 9, 1993, p. 17.
14. *Ibid.*
15. See *Vanity Fair*, September 1993, pp. 74-80; and Paul Gigot, *Wall Street Journal*, May 28, 1993.
16. George Will, "Clintonism A Picture of Power-Grabbing, *Austin American-Statesman*, May 24, 1993, p. A9.
17. Hillary Clinton: See footnotes number 15 and 19 in this section.

18. Hillary Clinton "We Are All In This Together," *Newsweek*, February 15, 1993, p. 22.

19. Carroll Quigley: *Tragedy And Hope: A History of the World In Our Time* (New York: Macmillan and Co., 1966).

20. This was Hillary's strange "Politics of Meaning" address. The complete text of her speech was printed In *Tikkun* magazine, May/June 1993.

21. Albert L. Weeks, The Current "CommuNazi" Phenomenon, *Global Affairs*, Spring 1987, p. 139.

22. Marlin Maddoux, *Freedom Club Report* (Address: P.O. Box 30, Dallas, Texas 75221) August 1993, pp. 3-4.

23. Berit Kjos, "From the Counter-culture to the Earth Summit," *The Christian World Report*, June-July, 1992, p. 19.

24. *Ibid.*

Part Four   A New Age Goddess in the White House

1. Barbara Marx Hubbard, *The Hunger of Eve* (Eastsound, Washington: Island Pacific NW, 1989), pp. 8-9.

2. John Randolph Price, *Practical Spirituality* (Austin, Texas: Quartus Books, 1985), p. 20.

3. John Randolph Price, *Commission Update* (Report), Planetary Commission for Global Healing, Austin, Texas, March 1988, p. 4.

4. Monica Sjoo and Barbara Mor, *The Great Cosmic Mother* (San Francisco: Harper & Row, 1987), pp. 430-431.

5. Rosemary R. Reuther, *Womanguides: Readings Toward A Feminist Theology* (Boston: Beacon Press, 1985), p. 213.

6. Naomi Goldenberg, *Changing of the Gods* (Boston: Beacon Press, 1979).

7. *Ibid.*

8. Rosemary Reuther, quoted by Robert J. Hutchinson, "On the Left," *Catholic Twin Circle*," November 20, 1988, p. 10.

9. Madonna Kolbenschlag, quoted by Donna Steichen, "The Goddess Goes to Washington," *Fidelity*, December 1986, pp. 36-44.

10. *Ibid.*

11. Alexandra Kovats, "Reclaiming Serpent Power," *Creation*, September/October 1988.

12. David J. Meyer, Trumpet Ministries, Wisconsin, quoted in *The Reaper*, April 27, 1993, p. 4.

13. Jeannie Williams, *USA Today*, February 23, 1993, p. 20.

14. *Ibid.*

15. William Hoar, "Hillary Clinton: Another Eleanor?," *The New American*, February 22, 1993, p. 43. Also see the books, *Love, Eleanor*, by Joseph Lash, and *FDR: An Intimate History*, by Nathan Miller.

16. *Ibid.*

17. *Ibid.*

18. *Ibid.*

19. *Intercessors for America* (newsletter), July 1993.

20. *Newsweek*, October 26, 1992, p. 31.

21. *Christian News*, January 18, 1993, p. 8; March 1, 1993, p. 21; October 12, 1993 p. 9 and 15.

22. *Ibid.*

23. "A More Maternal God," *Time*, May 25, 1993.

Part Five   Bad Company

Patricia Achtenberg, Assistant Secretary of HUD

1. Suzanne Fields, "Enough 'In Your Face' Homosexuality," *Los Angeles Times Syndicate*, Times Mirror Square, Los Angeles 90053, June, 1993.

2. Dick Hafer, *Shafted: Bill and Hillary's Excellent Adventure*, p. 41.

3. *Ibid.*

4. *Newsweek*, June 7, 1993, p. 37.

Madeleine Albright, U.S. Ambassador to the UN

1. Private communication from a confidential source.

2. *The CFR Trilateral/New World Order Connection*, Fund to Restore an Educated Electorate, P.O. Box 33339, Kerrville, Texas 78029.

3. Carroll J. Quigley, *Tragedy and Hope: A History of the World in Our Time* (New York: Macmillan, 1966).

4. *Ibid.*

5. Charles A. Provan, *American Freedom Movement* (newsletter).

6. *Newsweek*, August 23, 1993, p. 17.

7. *Ibid.*

8. Franklin Sanders, *The Moneychanger*, (P.O. Box 341753, Memphis Tennessee 38184) February, 1993. Also reprinted in the *Bulletin* of The Committee to Restore the Constitution, Lt. Col. Archibald Roberts, AUS (retired), director (P.O. Box 986, Fort Collins, Colorado 80522).

9. Zbigniew Brzezinski, *Between Two Ages* (New York: Penguin Books, 1970).

Jane Alexander, Chairman, National Endowment for the Arts

1. Texe Marrs, *America Shattered* (Austin, Texas: Living Truth Publishers, Inc., 1991).

2. Cliff Kincaid, "Exposing the NEA," *The New American*, September 6, 1993, p. 37.

3. *Ibid.* Also see "Turret of the Times," by *The Christian News*, July 6, 1992, p. 3.

4. Bill Clinton and Al Gore, *Putting People First: How We Can All Change America* (New York: Times Books, 1992) pp. 43-44.

5. *Newsweek*, August 9, 1993. Also see "Clinton Casts Actress Alexander for NEA Role," by Charles Storch (*Knight-Ridder Tribune New Service*), *Austin American-Statesman*, August 8, 1993, p. A19.

6. *Ibid.*

Maya Angelou, Inaugural Poet

1. "Clinton Gala to Feature Noteworthy Musicians" (*Associated Press*), *Austin American-Statesman*, January 7, 1993, p. A4. Also see "Clintons Attend Activist Reception," by Carol Ness (*San Francisco Examiner*), *Marietta, Georgia Daily Journal*, December 15, 1992.

2. See Paul West, "The Clinton Inauguration" (*Baltimore Sun*), *Austin American-Statesman*, January 21, 1993, p. A12.

3. Barbara Reynolds, "Maya Angelou: Silent No More," *USA Today*, January 18, 1993, p. 13A.
4. "Moment of Creation," *People*, January 18, 1993, pp. 62-63.
5. Carol Lynn Grossman, "The Search For a Haven of the Spirit," *USA Today*, December 15, 1992, p. D1.
6. Michael Toms, "Maya Angelou: A Poet's Progress," *Magical Blend*, pp. 30-36.
7. *Ibid.*
8. Texe Marrs, *Circle of Intrigue: Bill Clinton and The Plot to End American Sovereignty* (Austin, Texas: Living Truth Publishers, 1994).
9. Texe Marrs "Inaugural Weirdness: Bill Clinton Takes Americans Into "The Twilight Zone," *Flashpoint* newsletter (1708 Patterson Road, Austin, Texas 78733), February, 1993, pp. 1-2.
10. Marilyn Millay, "Angelou's Poem Is For the People" (*Newsday*), *Austin American-Statesman*, January 21, 1993, p. A12.
11. *Ibid.*
12. *Ibid.*
13. *Ibid.*
14. *Ibid.*
15. "Critic of Black Inaugural Poet Sued By University," *American Information Newsletter* (Box 44534, Boise, Idaho 83711), pp. 7-8.
16. John Meroney, "The Real Maya Angelou," *The American Spectator*, March 1993, p. 68.
17. *Ibid.*
18. *Ibid.*
19. Barbara J. Walker, "*The Woman's Dictionary of Symbols and Sacred Objects*" (San Francisco: Harper & Row Publishers, 1988), p. 63.
20. Maya Angelou, *Now Sheba Sings The Song* (New York: E.P. Dutton, 1987).
21. *Ibid.*
22. *Ibid.*
23. *Ibid.*
24. *Ibid.*
25. *Ibid.*
26. Maya Angelou's endorsement is printed in the brochure, "Your Voice Against Tolerance," published by the *People For the American Way Action Fund*.
27. BURR press release, February 15, 1993. For a detailed, but tragic, account of the ungodly, corrupt, and ultra-liberal goings-on at the National Religious Broadcasters International convention in 1993, see the article, "Televangelists Singin' the Blues," by Sara Diamond, in *Z* magazine, April, 1993.

Carol Bellamy, Director of the Peace Corps
1. *USA Today*, July 1, 1993, p. 6A.
2. *Washington Post*, April 15, 1993, p. 4.

Carol Browner, Head of Environmental Protection Agency
1. Franklin Sanders, *The Moneychanger*, February, 1993.
2. Two excellent books outlining the evironmental scam and its connection to the New World Order conspiracy are *Global Tyranny: Step By Step*, by William F. Jasper (Western Islands, P.O. Box 8040, Appleton, Wisconsin 54913); and *Sound and Fury: The Science and Politics of Global Warming* (Washington, D.C.: Cato Institute, 1992).

3. Thomas Eddlem, "Audubon Attack," *The New American*, September 6, 1993, p. 19.

4. Don McAlvany, as quoted in *The Evangelical Methodist*, Vol. 72, March 1993, p. 7 (Note: Address for *The McAlvany Intelligence Advisor is: P.O. Box 84904, Phoenix, Arizona 85071*).

Joycelyn Elders, Surgeon General of the United States

1. Charles A. Provan, *The American Freedom Movement Newsletter*, August 1993, pp. 3-4.

2. *Ibid.*

3. Billy James Hargis, "Dr. Joycelyn Elders' Nomination Shows Clinton's Contempt," *Christian Crusade* (Address: P.O. Box 977, Tulsa, OK 74102), August 1993, pp. 1-7. Also see "Joycelyn Elders us. Good Health," by William N. Grigg, *The New American*, September 20, 1993; "Arrogance That Blinds," by Paul Greenberg, *Washington Times*, July 28, 1993, p. G1; and "Dr. Elders' Record in Arkansas," *Wall Street Journal*, July 22, 1993. p. A14.

4. *Rush Limbaugh Show* (television), July, 1993.

5. Hargis, *op. cit.*

6. *Ibid.*

7. *Ibid.*

8. *Ibid.*

9. *Log Cabin Democrat*, 1991.

10. *The Reaper*, August 4, 1993; and see *Wall Street Journal*, July 22, 1993.

11. Hargis, *op. cit.*

12. See footnote number 3 above.

13. *Ibid.* Also, "Talk Live," NBC-TV, June 19, 1993.

14. *Ibid.*

15. See footnote number 3 above.

16. *Ibid.*

17. *Wall Street Journal*, July 22, 1993.

18. *Ibid.*

19. *Ibid.* And see footnote number 3.

20. *Ibid.*

21. *Ibid.*

22. *Ibid.*

23. *Ibid.*

24. Susan Fields, *Los Angeles Times Syndicate*, 1993.

25. See footnote number 3 above.

26. *Ibid.*

27. *Ibid.*

28. *Ibid.*

29. *Ibid.*

30. *Ibid.*

31. *Ibid.*

32. *Ibid.*

33. Wanda Marrs, "Peace Links" Goal Is One World Government," *Flashpoint*, February, 1990, p. 2.

34. *USA Today*, July 28, 1993.

35. Henry Foster, Jr., *Nashville Banner*, 1993.
36. See footnote number 3 above.
37. *Ibid.*
38. *Ibid.*
39. *Ibid.*
40. *Ibid.*
41. Joan Beck, "Elders' Policies on Teenage Sex Cause for Concern (*Chicago Tribune*), For The People News Reporter, August 23, 1993, p. 14.

Ruth Bader Ginsburg, Supreme Court Justice
1. *USA Today*, July 29, 1993, p. 10A.
2. *Austin American-Statesman*, June 15, 1993, p. 1.
3. *Newsweek*, June 28, 1993, p. 29.
4. R.E. McMaster, *The Reaper*, June 30, 1993, p. 10.
5. *Ibid.*
6. R.E. McMaster, *The Reaper*, May 19, 1993, p. 14.
7. *Human Events*, July 3, 1993.
8. Charles A. Provan, *The American Freedom Movement* (newsletter), August, 1993, p. 3.
9. "No Place for Homophobia," *San Francisco Sentinental*, March 26, 1992.
10. Demand #7, under the "Civil Rights" category, of the 55 demands for the 1993 March on Washington (*Washington Blade*, May 22, 1992). Also see *Christian World Report*, August, 1993, p. 19.
11. *The Evangelical Methodist*, April, 1993, p. 5.
12. "Senate to Close Part of Ginsburg Hearings," *USA Today*, July 16, 1993, p. 4A.
13. *Prophecy in the News* (Address: 1145 Southwest 74th Street, Oklahoma City, OK 73139) August, 1993, p. 3.
14. *Christian American*, February, 1993, p. 18.
15. *Grapevine Publications Network*, August/September 1993. Also see *Summit Journal*, May, 1993.

Tipper Gore, Wife of the Vice President
1. Letter from Senator Albert Gore to Representative Henry Hyde. I have a copy of this letter in my files.
2. "Jerry Garcia and The Grateful Dead: The Road Goes on Forever," *Rolling Stone*, September 2, 1991, pp. 42-46, 76-77.
3. *Ibid.*
4. *Ibid.*, p. 76.
5. *Ibid.*
6. *USA Today*, April 7, 1993, p. 3A.
7. Reported in *The Reaper*, R.E. McMaster, editor, May 19, 1993, p. 12.

Hazel O'Leary, Secretary of Energy
1. Franklin Sanders, *The Moneychanger*, February, 1993.
2. *The Washington Spectator*, April 1, 1993, p. 3.
3. *Ibid.*

Tara O'Toole, Assistant Secretary of Energy

1. Clifford Krauss, "Feminist Affiliation May Thwart Energy Nominee" (*New York Times News Service*), *Austin American-Statesman*, July 17, 1993.
2. *Ibid.*
3. *Ibid.*
4. *Ibid.*

Janet Reno, Attorney General

1. Dick Hafer, *Shafted: Bill and Hillary's Excellent Adventure* (A.K.A., Inc., P.O. Box 5401, Falmouth, Virginia 22403, 1993), p. 45.
2. *Washington Post*, April 21, 1993, p. B8.
3. *Ibid.*
4. *Miami Herald*, February 10, 1993.
5. "Hope for America in Honest AG," *Spotlight*, March 1, 1993.
6. *Ibid.*
7. *Ibid.*
8. *Ibid.*
9. *Ibid.*
10. As reported by the Associated Press and Republic Wire Services.
11. *Washington Times*, March 31, 1993, p. G1.
12. *Ibid.*
13. *Ibid.*
14. *Ibid.*
15. See *The Messenger* (Austin, Texas), May 5, 1993, Vol. 6, No. 9, p. 1. Also see *The New York Guardian*, April, 1993.
16. *Ibid.*
17. *Ibid.*
18. *Ibid.*
19. Charles A. Provan, *American Freedom Movement Newsletter*, April, 1993, p. 7. Also see the following sources: *Chronicles* (published by the Rockford Institute), April, 1993; "Is Janet Reno A Lesbian?," by Rev. Robert L. Slimp, *The Christian News*, February 22, 1993; "Finally, An Attorney General," *The New American*, April 19, 1993; "Janet Reno A Lesbian?," *Wisconsin Report*, March 4, 1993, page 3; "More on Janet Reno," by Franklin Sanders, *Moneychanger*, March 1993; "Is Florida Attorney John Thompson a Slanderer?," by David Becker, *The Christian News*, March 29, 1993, page 17; and "Hillary Selects Lesbian as Attorney General," by Larry Patterson, *Criminal Politics*, February 1993.
20. *Ibid.*
21. *Ibid.*
22. *Ibid.*
23. *Ibid.*
24. *Ibid.*
25. *Ibid.*
26. *Ibid.*
27. *Ibid.*
28. *Ibid.*
29. *Ibid.*
30. *Ibid.*

31. For accurate accounts of the Waco massacre (as opposed to the disinformation and outright lies and propaganda of the Reno/Clinton cabal), I recommend the following sources: "Waco Incident Could Happen Despite Gun Laws," by Paul Craig Roberts, *The Forum* (published by Eagle Forum, Colorado), Summer 1993, p. 6; "ADL Firmly Linked to Waco Tragedy," *Spotlight*, May 17, 1993; *News Reporter* (published by Chuck Harder's "For the People"), May 3, 1993, pp. 1-3; "Waco Raid Inquiry Reveals ATF Errors," by Pierre Thomas (*Washington Post Service*), *Austin American-Statesman*, August 14, 1993, p. A26; "Waco: An Unnecessary Tragedy," *The New American*, May 17, 1993; "ATF Brass Deflect Criticism, Defend Actions in Cult Standoff," by Neil Orman, *Houston Chronicle*, April 23, 1993; *The Watchman*, Summer 1993; "Experts Unraveling Mystery of Cult Standoff, Deaths," by Michael Landsberg (*Associated Press*), *Austin American-Statesman*, May 14, 1993, p. A14; "Some Wonder At Necessity of Raid on Cults," by Mark Post, *USA Today*, March 5, 1993; "About April 19th," *Intel Page*, Region Five Report, Vol. #5, Issue #5, p. 8; "Koresh Follower to Give Himself Up," by David Bond, *Bonner County Daily Bee* (Bonner County, Idaho), April 22, 1993; "Showdown in Waco," by Louis Beam, *The Jubilee*, March/April 1993--also see May/June and July/August issues; "David Koresh: He Said He Was King of the Jews," audiotape by Texe Marrs, Living Truth Ministries, Austin, Texas 78733; "Amongst the Ashes," *Time*, May 10, 1993; "God's Messenger," by Haim Shapiro, *The Jerusalem Post International Edition*, July 17, 1993, pp. 12B-12C; "News Update: Waco Texas," by John C. Torell, *The Dove*, Summer 1993; "Did CAN and the ADL Sucker the Feds Into April 19 Massacre?," by Harvey Schlanger, *The New Federalist*, May 3, 1993; "Waco Burn-Out Polarizes Americans," S.A. Freeman, editor, *The Citizen's Claw*, May 1993; *Waco: The Big Lie*, a video narrated by Linda Thompson, American Justice Federation; "Remember Waco," by James Knox, *American Focus*, April 20, 1993; "Recent Waco Tragedy is Clinton's Apocalypse," by Jeffrey Hart, *Minden (La.) Press-Herald*, May 1993. Also see the *Search Warrant* issued by the United States District Court, Western District of Texas, #W93-15M.

32. *Ibid.*

33. *Ibid.* Also see "Lethal Fumes," by Robert W. Lee, *The New American*, June 28, 1993.

34. *Ibid.* Also, see sources cited above for footnote No. 31.

35. *Ibid.*

36. "Restudying Waco," *Newsletter From A Christian Ministry*, Fritz Springmeir, publisher, June 1, 1993, p. 44.

37. Herb Brin, *Heritage* (Los Angeles, California), 1993.

38. Alexander Cockburn, "From Salem to Waco by Way of the Nazis," *Los Angeles Times*, April 27, 1993.

39. *Ibid.*

40. *Ibid.*

41. *Ibid.*

42. *Ibid.*

43. *Ibid.*

44. *Ibid.*

45. John Ed Pearce, "Ethnic Cleansing: Texas Style," *The Courier-Journal* (Indiana), April 1993.

46. *Ibid.*

47. *Ibid.*

48. Vic Fazell, quoted by R.E. McMaster, editor, *The Reaper*, April 14, 1993, p. 14.

49. See sources cited above for footnote No. 31.

50. *Ibid.*

51. David Koresh, quoted by Associated Press and in newspapers across the U.S.A.

Margaret Richardson, IRS Commissioner
1. "Powerful Friends of Hillary (FOH)," *Newsweek*, July 19, 1993, p. 6.
2. Robert W. Lee, "A Law Unto Itself," *The New American*, May 17, 1993, pp. 65-66.
3. *Ibid.*
4. *Ibid.*
5. *Ibid.*

Alice Rivlin, Deputy Director, Office of Management and Budget
1. *Council on Foreign Relations Annual Report*, 1991.
2. See *Dark Majesty*, by Texe Marrs (Austin, Texas: Living Truth Publishers, 1993).
3. James P. Tucker, Jr., "One-Worlders Made Advances in '92," *Spotlight*, January 4, 1993, p. 9.
4. Franklin Sanders, *The Moneychanger*, February, 1993.
5. R.E. McMaster, *The Reaper*, April 14, 1993, p. 11.
6. *Ibid.*
7. Fritz Springmeier, *A Newsletter from a Christian Ministry*, 5316 Lincoln Street, Portland, OR 97215, "Financial Control of the World By Destruction of the Economy," May 15, 1993, p. 35.

Donna Shalala, Secretary of Health and Human Services
1. *C-Span*, April 25, 1993.
2. Eleanor Clift, "Clinton's Cabinet: Beyond White Men," *Newsweek*, December 21, 1992. Also see *Newsweek*, July 19, 1993, p. 6.
3. Connie Zhu, "Queen Shalala Mounts HHS Throne," Christian American, March, 1993, p. 12.
4. *Ibid.* Also see *Shafted: Bill and Hillary's Excellent Adventure*, by Dick Hafer, p. 44; *Human Events*, January 23, 1993; and "Shalala Faces Questions on 'Politically Correct' Issue," by Julia Malone (*Cox News Service*), *Austin American-Statesman*, January 10, 1993, p. A7.
5. *Ibid.*
6. Connie Zhu (see footnote 3 above).
7. *Heterodoxy*, April, 1992.
8. Julia Malone (see footnote 4 above).
9. *Ibid.*
10. *Ibid.*
11. *Ibid.*
12. "Clinton's Appointments," *Jerusalem Post International Edition*, January 20, 1993, p. 6.
13. Julia Malone (see footnote 4 above).
14. *Ibid.*
15. *Heterodoxy*, April, 1992.
16. Connie Zhu (see footnote 3 above).
17. "New Clinton Humanities Czar Favored Speech Suppression," *American*

Information Newsletter, May, 1993, pp. 1-2; also see *Christian Crusade*, June 1993, p. 9.

18. *Ibid.*

19. *Ibid.*

20. Franklin Sanders, *The Moneychanger*, February, 1993.

21. *Human Events*, January 23, 1993, p. 1.

22. William F. Jasper, "Introduction to the Palace Guard," *The New American*, February 22, 1993, p. 37.

23. *The End Times and Victorious Living* (Address: Paw Creek Ministries, WPC, P.O. Box 668965, Charlotte, NC 28266), edited by Dr. Joseph Chambers, June/July, 1993. Illustration from *Life Advocate* (Address: P.O. Box 13656, Portland, Oregon 97213) February, 1993, pp. 4-6.

Laura D'Andrea Tyson, Chairman of the Council of Economic Advisors

1. Franklin Sanders, *The Moneychanger*, February, 1993.

2. Charles A. Provan, *The American Freedom Movement* (newsletter), August, 1993.

3. *Ibid.*

4. Fritz Springmeier, *A Newsletter From A Christian Ministry*, May 15, 1993, p. 35.

5. *Ibid.*

6. "Asides," *Wall Street Journal*, June 16, 1993.

7. *Ibid.*

Sheila Widnall, Secretary of the Air Force

1. Connie Cass "Nominee to Lead Air Force Soars in Male-dominated Field" (*Associated Press*), *Austin American-Statesman*, July 29, 1993, p. A2).

2. *Ibid.*

For Our Newsletter

Texe Marrs offers a *free* newsletter about Bible prophecy and world events, secret societies, the New Age Movement, cults, and the occult challenge to Christianity. If you would like to receive this newsletter, please write to:

Living Truth Ministries
1708 Patterson Road
Austin, Texas 78733-6507

About the Author

Well-known author of the #1 national bestseller, *Dark Secrets of The New Age*, **Texe Marrs** has also written 30 other books for such major publishers as Simon & Schuster, John Wiley, Prentice Hall/Arco, Stein & Day, and Dow Jones-Irwin. His books have sold over a million copies.

Texe Marrs was assistant professor of aerospace studies, teaching American defense policy, strategic weapons systems, and related subjects at the University of Texas at Austin for five years. He has also taught international affairs, political science, and psychology for two other universities. A graduate *summa cum laude* from Park College, Kansas City, Missouri, he earned his Master's degree at North Carolina State University.

As a career USAF officer (now retired), he commanded communications-electronics and engineering units. He holds a number of military decorations, including the Vietnam Service Medal, and served in Germany, Italy, and throughout Asia.

President of Living Truth Publishers in Austin, Texas, Texe Marrs is a frequent guest on radio and TV talk shows throughout the U.S.A. and Canada. His monthly newsletter, *Flashpoint*, is distributed around the world.